LESSONS FROM A

SMALL TOWN

A LOVE LETTER TO MY SOUTH

BILL THOMPSON

ISBN: 978-1-960146-61-8 (hard cover)
       978-1-960146-62-5 (soft cover)

Thompson. Bill

Edited by: Amy Ashby
and Mary Best

Cover photo by: Doug Sasser, South Wind Photography

PipeVine
P R E S S

Published by PipeVine Press
Charlotte, NC
www.warrenpublishing.net
Printed in the United States

A small town is a place where folks care
about you—whether you want 'em to or not.

Just Down the Road

L isten to poems and stories from this book on Bill's album *Just Down the Road* or online at www.southboundwithbillthompson.com. Set to original music and recited by author, speaker, and performer Bill Thompson, these beautiful and poignant poems are like a fresh glass of sweet tea enjoyed on Grandma's back porch—a soothing and satisfying taste of the South.

Table of Contents

INTRODUCTION

As a part of my semiquarantine routine during the pandemic, I reread many books that are stored on the shelves in my office. I couldn't buy new ones or check out (hardly) anything from the library, so I read what I had. There were two old publications that resonated with me as the tribulations we had been facing with the pandemic and racial unrest reverberated.

The first was set in the South, my home. In William Faulkner's *Absalom! Absalom!*, Quinton Compson's Harvard classmate asks, "Tell about the South. What's it like down there. What do they do there. Why do they live there. Why do they live at all."

The other is a play by Thornton Wilder set in New Hampshire in the imaginary town of Grover's Corners. That play is *Our Town*, one almost all of us have read or been a part of in a high school production.

Both books paint a timeless portrait of life in small-town, rural America. Both were written about and in different times—times when the world was different, when we were different. Our lives are no longer tied to the land and the seasons. We don't talk over the backyard fence, tell stories around the woodstove at the general store, or write letters. But that sense of community is still alive in small Southern towns, that sense of belonging that is at the heart of who we are. We still long to talk with each other, to tell stories.

And the stories are timeless. They still address the personalities and culture of a part of America that certainly has changed but remains a unique community that has great promise, even if the promise is delayed. Readers or audience members can see a part of themselves if they are paying attention.

And I paid attention and thought I could get a better understanding of my own world if I could do something similar: paint a word picture of our current time and place in the small rural towns and communities across North Carolina and the rest of the South.

I am no Thornton Wilder or William Faulkner, but over the years, I have had a unique canvas on which to paint that portrait: the *News Reporter* in Whiteville and magazines such as *Our State*, *Garden and Gun*, and *Salt*, among others, along with my books. Part of my job at the *News Reporter* is to write about the people and places in Columbus County. I write a series called *Where Are They Now?* that enables me to track down those folks who have made contributions to our lives here and elsewhere but have retired or moved away. Finding those folks and telling their stories provides a history that is not available anywhere else.

But it is history.

What about the present? Who are we now? How will we be perceived in the future? What we do today is tomorrow's history. Just as the play *Our Town* does, I want to portray what is happening now on the living stage that is this South, My South. My role is the stage manager, the narrator. (In *Our Town* these are the same person.)

An irate lady told me the other day that Columbus County is an "evil Mayberry." I believe that is an oxymoron if there ever were one. Like every portrait, there are myriad colors and hues, shadows and light, angles and circles in the picture of this area, this place we call home. Without getting into a discussion of what constitutes art, I'll just modify the old cliché: "Art is in the eye of the beholder." I wanted to behold a bright, realistic picture of who we are. I wanted to go into each community and ask the residents who they think they are. I wanted to record my impressions of the everyday things that we sometimes take for granted, the new and the old, those living and those dying, that which is mundane and that which is celebratory.

A phrase I've heard many times as we greet newcomers to our area is, "Now, who are your people?" I wanted to answer that question. I don't mean just who are our ancestors, but what kind of people live here now, as well as those who have passed on. Why are you still here? What is your life like? Why do you do the work you do? Why do you go to that church or any church at all? What is your tie to this place, to these people? I wanted to answer the question posed to Quinton Compson; I wanted to look at the everyday things that we take for granted and show how important they really are.

The best analogy of what I intend to write is taken from *Our Town*'s heroine, Emily Webb, when she has died while giving birth and is given the chance to go back to any day in her life. She chooses her twelfth birthday.

I chose an ordinary day in each community. For good or bad, the days were during the COVID-19 pandemic. As a result, much of what I observed was seen in the shadow of the quarantine and the subsequent rules, regulations, and protocols. It gave a realistic view of the contemporary community of the county, but it went beyond the physical boundaries of sickness and lockdown to embrace My South. I believe that what I observed went beyond the cloud of the pandemic and looked at those universal traits that make us who we are as Southerners.

If you saw me driving around the community all day or asking people nosy questions, I wasn't "up to no good." I was gathering paint for the portrait of more than just the small point of Earth. I've created a portrait that is universal, a picture that I hope the reader can see of a time and place that is ever changing but constant in its appeal of "down home," a place where real people experience routine celebrations of who they are—who we are.

Columbus County is a specific place, and there are some characteristics unique to it. But this county also is representative of so many other communities throughout My South. The land and the climate are the same, and the tie to the land is the same, but how those elements affect the people who live there may vary. Nevertheless, the sense of "being Southern" is still there.

PART I
HOME'S NOT A PLACE; IT'S A STATE OF MIND

LISTENING TO A CAROLINA SUNRISE

You ever listened to a Carolina sunrise? A Tar Heel boy like me can. He doesn't have to hear it to listen to it; it speaks to his heart. First, there's the sun coming out of the ocean off the Outer Banks on a bright summer morning and the wind blowing the sea grass just enough to remind him of how that girl's hair looked on the beach yesterday. Even in the sunlight, there still lingers a memory of music wafting through the night sky, his fingers touching her fingers as they danced to the music.

He can smell the salt air, maybe even detect that distinctive but not really unpleasant funk that tells him it's low tide on the sound side. As the sun rises, so rises the anticipation of another day at the beach.

Then there's that other sunrise in a Carolina boy's soul, the one he sees across the top of a tobacco field. The mist rises to meet the sun looming over the textured dark-green expanse flanked by tall pines. An aroma of tobacco gum and pine rosin, the dusky smell of dust still damp with the dew of late summer fills the air. The breeze carries that Carolina perfume of tobacco curing in the barn beyond the trees.

Another sunrise is the glow of a new day spreading across the top of the mountains; low clouds and morning fog mingle with the smoke of chimney fires as the shadows of the night give way to the light of day. Even in the summer, the coolness requires a coat or sweater to keep a body from shivering while the sight of a mother bear and her cub warms the soul.

(Listen to Bill recite this poem at www.southboundwithbillthompson.com.)

Just Down the Road

I listen to the South Wind as it talks and sings.
It plays its melodies through the pine trees,
whispers on the beaches and creeks
and screams over the mountain tops.

The poet listens to it all,
It's the sound of you and me,
Of farmers and store clerks,
And those who used to be.
It's the heartbeat of our being,
A plea to keep us free,
For tomorrow comes a-rollin'
On each wave that leaves the sea.

Real Nostalgia

Last week I was filling up my car at Go Gas when a vehicle pulled up on the other side of the pump I was using. Turned out, the driver was an old friend of mine I had not seen since our college days more than fifty years ago. We didn't look like we did back then, but we began to talk as if we had just gotten out of chapel on the campus there in Buies Creek. But, as everybody knows, you can't spend time chatting at the gas pumps at Go Gas, so we only had a few minutes together.

After I left the pumps and headed home, I got to thinking, as I often do, of how much things have changed around here since my friend and I went off to school more than half a century ago. Many of my thoughts are nostalgic reveries, recollections of the past, often sentimental reflections. I have to remind myself sometimes that nostalgia is just edited memory. We tend to leave out the bad things or look at them from that long-ago perspective that softens the image.

But once my mind goes into reverse gear, it's hard to stop it. After all, I can see a whole lot more behind me than I can see in front of me, and the present is ephemeral, instantly becoming the past.

But on that nostalgic journey, I began thinking about the things that had not changed—those verities, some physical, some cultural, some parts of my life and as permanent as tombstones.

As I drove across that stretch of swamp between White Marsh and Whiteville, I noticed it had changed. Not too long ago, the whole swamp was full of trees. But a dry spell came along that enabled logging equipment to get in the normally wet area, and almost all that old cypress that had been there so long was gone. But the swamp is still there, and every time it rains, the water rises to the edge of the road—and sometimes over it—and I see sprouts on the cypress stumps. The egrets and herons still walk through the shallow water like elegant, awkward dancers. And the cold winter wind blows across the swamp grass and lily pads, and the gray moss hangs like ancient beards from cypress trees next to the road. Some things don't change.

I followed the highway on down to Lake Waccamaw and turned right on Flemington Drive, crossed over where the railroad track used to be and down the street that was once sheltered with pecan limbs that made a leafy tunnel down to the lake shore. Those trees are gone now, but the remnant of the pecan orchard of which those roadside trees were a part is still standing on the Boys and Girls Homes campus. Down on the shore of the lake, Miss Carrie Weaver's pier and pavilion are gone now—as are the boardwalk along the shore and the old bathhouses.

But the lake is still there, and the water still laps on the sandy shore, and motorboats and sailboats still glide and skip over the waves. When summer comes, the humidity and heat force homeowners and visitors to seek out private piers and the wildlife park where they cook hamburgers and hot dogs and play in the shallow water. On the swamp side and along the canal, turtles line up on fallen logs, forming a buffet table for alligators. Some things never change.

I drive past old tobacco barns, falling wooden remnants of a time when everybody's life was tied in some way to the sticky green plants that grew on almost every farm. There is no use for those barns anymore. But there are round metal storage bins, some full of corn, some full of soybeans or oats. The fields are now covered in winter stubble, but soon they'll be tilled and planted, and next fall, the farmers will harvest them again. The land and the farmer and the seasons are still tied together. Some things never change.

As I come back into Hallsboro, the nostalgia really hits me. All the old lumber mills are gone. All the little businesses that sustained me through my youth: Miss Ellis's ice cream shop, Mr. Penny and Mr. Baldwin's barber shop, the old movie theater, Claude Pierce's store and Mr. J.B. Council's garage, Miss Callie Hayes's store, McNeil's cleaners, Thurman's garage, my family's store, Council and Company, the train depot ... all gone.

My wife told me to stop at Pierce and Company and get some sausage for breakfast. I did. Inside the store is unedited nostalgia.

Some things never change.

Pierce and Co. Has New Owners

For only the second time in its 120-year history, Pierce and Co. is under new ownership. The iconic business was purchased by Mark and Sarah Bronski. The young couple and their family formerly lived in Connecticut before moving back to Sarah's home county. She is the daughter of Susan and William Wood of Whiteville.

"All the time I lived here, I never went into the store," she says. "Of course, we drove by, going back and forth from the lake to Whiteville, but we never stopped." But on a recent visit, she and her husband decided to stop and immediately "fell in love with the place."

"I immediately liked what I saw," Mark says. "This is a unique business, an institution in this community, and when we heard it was for sale, we knew we wanted to be a part of it. We don't plan to make any changes. We may look at some new marketing plans, but the company will stay the same. It will still be Pierce and Co., and we want to continue to build on that heritage that has made it what it is today."

The couple met while they were in Germany working for an international engineering firm, the Trump Co. (no relation to the former president), with more than fourteen thousand employees around the world. Their friendship continued when they returned to the corporate office in Connecticut, and they were married in 2012. Now, ten years later, they have moved south with their two children, Anna and Henry, settled into temporary residence at Lake Waccamaw, and started on their new life together in a much different environment.

The Bronskis purchased the business, named after its primary investor, Mr. Pierce, from William and Brenda Jolly and Thomas and Gail Jolly in 2020, who purchased it in 1990 from the founding Wyche family. The current store was built about 1923, when the business was moved from the original store at Red Bug, a community just a few miles south of Hallsboro.

William Jolly says: "We thought it was time to make a change, for us to move on, and we wanted to pass the torch to the next generation. We wanted somebody who shared our appreciation for the past and the current role the company plays in this community. Mark and Sarah bring that appreciation and their own particular background in the modern business world to Pierce and Co. We are optimistic about the future of the business."

No changes have taken place nor are any planned in the future for operation of the company. Gary Hooks will remain as manager and David Hooks as assistant manager. The other employees also will remain in their current positions.

In his first week as president of Pierce and Co., Mark made an effort to get to know not only his employees but also his customers. As many of the regulars come in, he introduces himself, or one of the employees will make the introduction. The usual response is: "Well, welcome. Hope you don't change much."

The venerable mercantile company has survived and prospered by meeting the needs of the local community. That is what Mark plans to continue. "We want to listen to our customers and respond to their needs," he says. "We want them to feel as comfortable coming in here as they always have. We will still have the diverse inventory, still have the custom meat market, and still provide the hardware and lumber just like it has always been." Mark mentions when they were doing some work on their Lake Waccamaw house, someone told them to call Pierce and Co. and order the materials they needed, and they would be delivered. "They not only brought exactly what I wanted but delivered it in less than an hour and helped unload it! Where else does that happen?" he says.

Mark also notes the tremendous amount of traffic caused by folks passing through Hallsboro on their way to the beach. "I saw a lot of people stop to buy meat and other items on the way to spend the weekend or vacation at the beach. That is another unique aspect of this store. And almost everybody 'just passing through' wants to look at the store. They ask about the old floors and stamped-tin ceiling and the Radio Flyer wagons and the handmade bird houses. It's an educational experience. There's not another place like it, and people are amazed to find it ... and they'll be back!"

The new owner of Pierce and Co. has already learned something that longtime residents know: sometimes it's the old that is new.

BYRDVILLE

Travelers going east in the morning might be blinded by the rising sun and miss the sign by the side of NC 74/76 that reads "Byrdville." As they take that road to the south, make a right turn by the recycling site, and carry on down the paved country road, they might be distracted by the folks unloading refuse. It is familiar territory to anybody who grew up in this part of the country: green pastures with old barns—some still showing the ravages of storms, their tin roofs hanging precariously in the morning light. There are newer barns too and sturdy new homes just past a pasture with a mobile home that sits in the dent made by the pasture fence.

Lot of folks out this way are involved in the trucking business. The big rigs sit beside the dwellings. Some of the big engines idle like workhorses poised to take to the road. Some will be gone and back before dark; others won't be back for several days.

The summer sun creeps slowly to the top of the pine trees along the road, casting long shadows that fold like fingers pulling the road closer to the sunrise. Just a mile or two down that Byrdville road, a man and a boy are working on a truck. The truck and other equipment are parked under a large metal building, and beside it is a large brick home.

Phil Grice is a trucker. He hauls salt every day from Wilmington to Hamlet, where it is used in a process to make fumigants for farming and other products as well.

The young assistant, Carter Bigford, lives just down the road. "Thinks he's family," Phil says with a smile. The two continue working as this visitor inquires about the status of Byrdville. "Yep, this is home. Raised right down there in that building you can see from here," he says, pointing toward a white frame building just a short distance north of his house. "That used to be the old Byrdville school, but my family made it into a house, and all my family was raised there," he adds.

"Lived here all my life. Not much changes. The biggest change has been getting paved roads. I'm sixty-four years old, and I remember when Mr. Dowless got killed when he ran his '54 Ford into the bridge railing right after the road was paved. We weren't used to being able to go that fast on these roads.

"Started working at the old Amoco station when I was a boy. Got interested in trucking and got into that business," he explains.

When asked if he was an apprentice trucker, Carter says, "No, going to get more education first, then I'll figure it out."

"Thankful for my life here," Phil says. "Family has been here for generations. Got a good wife. Got a farm too. Good neighbors. Got another house down at the beach we go to 'bout every weekend. Lots of churches around here: Red Hill Pentecostal, Cheerful Hope Baptist, Livingston Baptist, some others. But since we're at the beach, that's where we go.

"Well, listen. I'd love to talk some more, but we got to get this job done. Come back and see me again, though, and we'll talk some more," he says.

Just past Phil's place are more farms. A pond with several goats grazing its edge shines in the morning sun now pushing its summer heat, causing a little mist to rise from the water that has been cooled by the night.

There are some small trees blown down on the side of the road, remnants of the previous night's storm. Lena Dale Road narrows from

Byrdville onto a dirt road with no name. The path is surprisingly dry, given the recent storm. A lone turkey ventures out in front of the woods into the path of the car and runs ahead—then wisely runs back into the woods. Finding himself on a logging road, the wary traveler doesn't enter private land without permission, so he turns around and heads back toward Byrdville.

The road now passes barren fields as well as fields of tall corn and oats. Newly built houses and several mobile homes are nestled between the fields in egalitarian tranquility.

There is a community cemetery on the right side of the road just before it reconnects back to Highway 74/76. It may have been a family cemetery that became a community cemetery. It is well-kept, the grass recently mowed and fresh flowers and artificial arrangements on some of the graves. There are familiar names on the tombstones: Alford, Connelly, Little, Mintz, Roberts. These are old names of families that have lived here for centuries. An American flag hangs limply in the midday sun, even as several smaller flags ripple softy at the graves of military veterans buried there.

There is one large tombstone with an epitaph noting that the body of the person placed there was named Rufus Alford. He was killed in France on September 18, 1918. The people of Byrdville and Freeman have been serving their country for a long time. If Rufus Alford and any of the others were to come back today, some things would have changed. But it would still be home.

Buckhead/St. James

Sunrise seems to be a busy time in Buckhead. Traffic on Old Lake Road is heavy. This road is the highway that bisects the community. It's the passageway for those going to work, for school buses, and for those folks going for breakfast down at The Corner Grill. The grill is a popular place in the community, particularly during deer hunting season when the hunters come by for breakfast and/or lunch. They talk about the trophies they shot or the one they missed. Donna Freeman, who is behind the counter and serving meals, says, "They eat a lot of bacon and eggs and always grits and drink a lot of coffee." The smell of food cooking adds to the camaraderie that comes when folks who have known each other for generations come together. It's a scene covered in camouflage, dotted with bright yellow caps and vests.

By midmorning, the diners have left, and a quiet serenity settles over the place. Maybe it's the presence of all the churches: Mt. Sinai Holiness, New Hope Baptist, Union Chapel, Shiloh Methodist, and others, including the namesake St. James, just a few miles down the road. Or maybe it's because the morning sun is lifting the mist from the fields, pastures, and woods, revealing an ancient land that is as much a part of Buckhead and St. James as the people who live here. It was the rivers and trees that brought the Old People—their ancestors—here hundreds of years ago. Though there are few who till the soil now, many of the Waccamaw Sioux and their neighbors still harvest the woodlands where their ancestors once hunted. Ironically, it was the White hunter that gave Buckhead its name. As hunting clubs formed, members would tell of the big bucks and place the habitant, the buck headquarters, between the Cape Fear River and Lake Waccamaw. The community may venture into the edge of Bladen County, but the address is Bolton.

This is a prosperous community. Trucking and construction companies sit beside fields of winter stubble from corn and soybeans, pastures with grazing cattle, and the replenishing woodlands cut over and already sprouting new growth. There is a tradition of continuity amongst the town's residents, a determination to remain here even if work takes them elsewhere. So, many find employment in Whiteville and Wilmington and Elizabethtown and Riegelwood. But they always return to Buckhead and St. James.

Brenda Moore is in her office this morning at the tribe's headquarters. It's a modern building, built by the tribe for the tribe and situated appropriately in the middle of the community. The headquarters is where the tribal council meets and where decisions are made on not only how to preserve native heritage but also to provide for the betterment of the community. Next door sits a community athletic field and a daycare center, and in front of it all is a giant wooden carving of a Native American, a monument to those who came before. The tribal grounds are the center for the annual powwow that celebrates the Waccamaw Siouxan heritage. But other activities take place here too. Former residents came back to teach computer classes to parents of students faced with the challenge of homeschooling due to the COVID-19 pandemic. Tribal members may move away, but they never really leave home. There is a food bank sponsored by American Indians, a proud nation.

Other traditions exist that many outside the community may not know about. For instance, when a tribal member dies, members of the community stay with the family all night before the funeral. The casket may be at the funeral home, but the Waccamaw Siouxan family is there for each other through the sorrow and grief.

Pam Jacobs is the current vice chair of the Waccamaw tribal council, part of the new generation to assume a leadership role and one of the few women to hold that office.

"There is a strong sense of community here," she says. "It is family. We take care of each other. Part of our goal is to pass on the heritage of our ancestors, but more importantly, we want to provide for the current and future needs of the community."

When asked why she is a part of all this, she says: "There is a great satisfaction in doing something good. I do it because it is right. We need to make sure that there will always be an appreciation and a pride in who we are. We are a part of the land. We know that there is a certain healing power in the land around us and need to make sure that we are not only aware of the power of the past but also the power of nature around us. It is not just the intangible pride but the tangible knowledge that there are certain real and healing values in nature, in God's creation, in green space, in the herbs and natural elements of the earth. They are real things that can heal our minds and our bodies. I want to be a part of that awareness in a real way, in a real world."

The goal of "taking care of each other" is most apparent in the Buckhead Fire and Rescue Department. The station is almost the geographic center of the community, as well as the center of community spirit. It is a modern, up-to-date facility staffed by well-trained volunteers. As darkness falls on this winter night, some of the fire and rescue members have gathered at the station. They join Angel Justice, who is the on-duty dispatcher for the night. Angel lives just a few miles toward Riegelwood, but she is a vital part of this operation.

Three young men join Angel at the station tonight, not for a station meeting nor even about the station but to talk about their community and why they are a part of it.

Nick Richardson is thirty years old, grew up in Buckhead, went to school at the old Hallsboro High School, and then attended the University of North Carolina at Pembroke. His day job is working for a tire company in Wilmington, but he still commits to his work in Buckhead. "It's home," he says. That statement is the rationale that every resident of Buckhead and St. James gives for their commitment to service. Home has a tie that binds them despite distance.

Austin Jacobs, just nineteen years old and the youngest of the group, has the same response. "It's home. There is a sense of community here. We are all family, and I like that. I like being a part of it."

Stefan Jacobs is the oldest of the young group at fifty-one. In the tribal parlance, he is an elder. He feels that same family connection. In fact, his father, Monroe Jacobs, ran a store that was the center of Buckhead for many years and still is run by his mother. The store is where local folks, Native American and White, converge almost every day to eat, drink soft drinks, and catch up on the local news.

Stefan graduated from Hallsboro High School, went off to college, got a degree in physics, and then came back to work with his father. "There is a cultural and spiritual sense of who we are. There was and still is, somewhat, a sense of being different," he says. "We not only accept that but embrace it even as we become more assimilated in the expanding world around us. Things may change here and elsewhere, but it will still be Buckhead, and it will still be home."

The night wind is snapping the American flag outside the fire station and pushing the clouds across the moon. To the south, toward Lake Waccamaw, a broad reflection of lightning flashes in the clouds, and the muffled sound of thunder rumbles softly. It will rain tonight on the fields and woods of Buckhead and St. James, and the sunshine will follow just as it has for hundreds of years. It's a tradition.

(Listen to Bill recite this poem, track number 7 on Just Down the Road.*)*

The Maiden of Lake Waccamaw

Some say the lake is an inland sea,
a spot where the ocean used to be.

Some say a star fell from the sky,
and water filled in where the hole was dry.
However it got there, it's a beautiful place,
full of beauty and history, home to a proud race
of people with a history so grand,
a heritage still tied to the land.

I rowed out on that lake one morn,
watched the sun rise up over the trees.
The lake was calm, hardly a breeze,
so I let my boat drift, didn't pick up an oar,
just drifted along 'til I lost sight of the shore.

Then out of the mist a figure appeared,
a soft wet image yet crystal clear.
She was seated on an island mound
with hundreds of flowers growing 'round.

She wore a beaded deer skin gown
that matched her own skin of brown.
Her braided black hair was hanging down,
and on top was a feathered crown.
Her eyes were closed like she was saying a prayer

while tears came rolling down,
and the rain fell all around.

I started rowing toward shore
already wet to the core.
But in a flash it was sunny and dry,
and the storm had passed me by.

And the maiden was gone,
and I sat there alone
surrounded by the clear blue sky.
And in my mind I wondered why
the maiden had appeared to me
in the middle of this inland sea.

I still don't know what the answer could be;
I guess I'll keeping trying to see.
I'll keep seeking the mysteries of life on this inland sea,
and when I find it, I'll just keep it right here
'tween the Indian maiden and me.

Evergreen

t is the first cool morning of the year. No frost yet, but the air is cool, and the breeze blowing across the intersection of Evergreen stirs memories as well as a few leaves that fall on the corner lot that could pass for a park or a town square in a bigger place. There's a young man walking with a little boy toward the school just west of the intersection. Maybe they're running behind schedule. As they walk down the street, the older of the two probably remembers the old store/gas station that once stood at that intersection. It burned a few years ago and hasn't been replaced. Since the store's incineration, folks in Evergreen say, "You can't even buy a Pepsi in Evergreen anymore." Indeed, there is not a commercial establishment in what is considered Evergreen unless you count Pait's Tractor over on the other side of Boardman and really in the Macedonia community.

The school that the man and little boy are headed to is about the most active building in the community except when the Fire and Rescue folks respond to an emergency or maybe on Sunday morning when the folks gather at one of the five churches for worship. There is a quiet peacefulness about the place that creates a contentment, a feeling that despite all the rancor and vitriol in the world around it, Evergreen is a good place to live.

The main intersection is where old US Route 74 crosses Highway 242. When the new I-74 was built, it bypassed Evergreen, taking with it all the traffic that might have come through and stopped for gasoline or

LESSONS FROM A SMALL TOWN: A LOVE LETTER TO MY TOWN

a snack. The only busy traffic area now is when school begins and ends each day.

If you walk through the cemeteries around Evergreen, including the one in front of the Baptist church, you'll see names like Britt, Griffin, Inman, Johnson, Kissam, Leggett, and Rabon, along with other names that have been a part of this community for generations. Unlike a lot of communities that have diminished over the years, these names are still prevalent, still on the church roles, still registered to vote or even run for office, still willing to lead even when there are few to lead.

Evergreen is one of those places that has prevailed despite the impingement of modernity. Some things may change just enough to maintain tradition. Folks still gather for church on Sunday mornings and some on Wednesday nights. But even that tradition has been affected by the COVID-19 pandemic. Still, some folks gather at the Methodist church right after lunch today to talk about their town, its past and present. Janice Johnson, Donald and Helen Leggett, and Patsy Christly have been a part of Evergreen for most, if not all, of their lives, teaching children about life along with their academic instruction.

Like other communities in the area, the current elegiac status doesn't reflect the real history. Longtime residents like those gathered at the church preface many of their remarks with, "There used to be ..." or "I remember when ..."—reflections on a past that only a few remember, much of it centered around the school, which is still a landmark.

A railroad ran through Evergreen until right after World War II. The thriving lumber business that was the basis of the economy in much of the county had begun to fade, and soon those lumber companies closed, and the primary occupation of folks in and around Evergreen was farming. A lot of folks also work in Lumberton and other areas nearby, making Evergreen a bedroom community.

Coming from the west side of town, a traveler is struck by the sight of a giant water oak, its dark presence dominating the skyline.

If he should stop by that tree, the visitor could perhaps hear the wind whisper through those old limbs and green leaves—and sounds of the sawmills, the laughter and conversation of the tobacco barns and fields, the cheering of the people as they watch the high school teams play basketball or baseball.

Baseball and Evergreen go together. If the town has a distinction nowadays, it has to be considered "Baseball Central" in Columbus County. Evergreen was one of the first communities to have its own semipro team in the years after World War II. The high school teams were always competitive. It was probably the Dixie Youth program that had the greatest impact. The late Bill Johnson was the Dixie Youth coach and one of the leaders of the county organization. Under Bill's guidance, as well as that of other coaches in the county, Columbus County Dixie Youth became an annual favorite to go to the national championship games. Many of the players went on to use their skills to get college scholarships, and others, like Evergreen natives Otis and Donell Nixon, went to the major leagues. Some folks say it is quite possible that Evergreen (and by extension, the county) has more major league baseball players per capita in its history than any other place in the country.

Baseball, school, church, farming, hunting, and fishing are some of the activities that designate Evergreen as a good place to live. Without taking a formal vote, the folks gathered at the Methodist church agree that they wouldn't want to live anywhere else.

Night takes its time settling on Evergreen. The chill of the early morning is returning as the sun sets over toward Boardman and the other side of that oak tree. The soft breeze that has wafted through the afternoon air has stilled. It is quiet in Evergreen. Wait! In the quiet of the night comes the familiar sound of a bat connecting with a baseball. Some memories still live.

Tabor City

I t's quiet in downtown Tabor City. It's not supposed to be. This is the weekend of the annual Yam Festival. This would have been the forty-ninth festival, but this year, 2020, the pandemic did what hurricanes and rainstorms and floods couldn't do. The parade was canceled—no beauty pageant and no Taste of Tabor, an outdoor garden party and feast. Although many of the traditional activities were called off, some others were held because of good management that had created surplus funds from previous celebrations. These included a virtual recipe contest, a decorating contest, and, of course, appearances by mascot Tiger Tater and a contest to decorate his hat.

A look down the railroad track that bisects the downtown doesn't reflect the lack of activities. The parking spaces are filled with early diners at Mama's Café, where there are no reservations but most of the seats are filled with the same people who sat in them yesterday morning. It's that kind of place where people come not just for the food but to visit, talking not only about the pandemic and the election but also who's sick, who has a new baby, and who has died.

Just down the street past the newly restored and renovated Ritz Theater, the same atmosphere exists at the Bluebyrd Café at lunchtime. Pam Byrd greets each costumer with a familiar "How y'all" and calls them by name. Chandler Worley and his wife have driven in from Fair Bluff to order the chicken bog, but it's not available today, so they settle for something else. Although the tables are separated more than usual to accommodate social distancing, conversation between tables continues. As more people come in, the noise increases, but nobody minds; they are all friends, and the noise accompanies the friendship.

"Remember when we used to put suds in the fountain in front of the bank?"

"We used to drive up and down the streets just to see who was in town on Saturday nights."

"I wish they weren't going to tear down the old school. Lots of memories in that building."

Pam is a primary mover to Bring Back Main, a chamber project that is aimed at renovating current businesses and getting new ones like Two Broke Teachers, an arts-and-crafts shop that just opened last year, to revitalize the downtown area.

Around the corner from the Bluebird Café is a landmark in transition. The Todd House began as a boarding house many years ago and was a favorite of tobacco buyers who would come to town when the tobacco market was open. They told others about the food and friendliness, and folks would come from long distances to eat there. For many folks, it was tradition to eat at the Todd House at least once a week. And every civic club in town held its meetings there. The Todd House isn't going away; it is, however, changing to form a new tradition.

Downtown Tabor City is like so many other small Southern towns. Businesses line both sides of the railroad track, and at the intersection of the two main streets stands the library. It's a great distinction for such a small town to have a library, and the fact that it sits in the middle of town is symbolic of its importance.

It's also symbolic that right beside the library is a little white building that would go almost unnoticed if it were not so busy. It is the office of the Tabor City Chamber of Commerce and the Yam Festival. Cynthia Nelson is director of the chamber, and Rachel Todd directs the North Carolina Yam Festival. From that small office, they promote Tabor City.

Down the street at the visitors center, Diane Nobles Ward not only welcomes visitors to the state and Tabor City but also works to attract business to the area. Tabor City is not a sleepy little Mayberry. To the contrary, it is full of small-town magic that people everywhere wish they could replicate. Of course, you can't copy Tabor City; you have to live there to appreciate it.

That appreciation is the very sentiment expressed by Mary Lou Molina. Before she and her husband moved down from New York, she had "all kinds of preconceptions" about the small-town, rural South, based on what they had read. They found those preconceptions to be misperceptions.

"I love it here!" she says as she sits in the horse barn at the center of Sunnyfield Farms, which she operates outside of town. In fact, Mary Lou loves Tabor City so much she became an active member of the Chamber of Commerce and is now its president. Last year she hosted the Taste of Tabor at the farm.

"Tabor City is like a country song," she says. "It is a great place to live, and I am so glad we found it. We really feel a part of the community. Folks just took us in and made us a part of them. We're the Yankees who stayed, and now we are home."

The dark of night begins to cover Tabor City, and the downtown lights come on, creating a scene that could have been in the classic movie *It's a Wonderful Life.* The atmosphere causes a visitor to reflect on what he has learned about the little town: small-town values, people who care about you, sharing and celebrating life together.

Williamson's Crossroads/Macedonia

Donna Godwin opens up Floyd's Country Store on an early Tuesday morning as tiny raindrops grow larger and the wind picks up a little. "I don't know if they're going to be able to get much tobacco in today," she says. She's talking about her husband, Kevin Godwin, and his crew of seven, who farm about fifty-eight acres of tobacco in the Williamson's Crossroads and Macedonia area of the county. Donna takes care of the store and Kevin works the fields.

The store was built by Donna's father, Bobby Floyd. Donna and Kevin bought it from him. But Donna is quick to add, "This will always be Floyd's Country Store." She was an educator in the Columbus County Schools for years, many as a teacher at nearby Evergreen Elementary School, and quite a few of her customers are former students. "It's like a class reunion almost every day," she laughs.

"When I first started teaching school, the superintendent wanted to know if I would be comfortable teaching in a community where I would know all the parents and even be teaching some of my family," she says. "My answer was an emphatic 'Yes.' Teaching, both academics and discipline, is much easier when I can simply address a problem with a candid personal call or conversation at church."

The Godwins have one son, two daughters, and one granddaughter, Baileyanna, who is not only the center of attention there in the store but is also the obvious center of their hearts as well. "This store is a part of who we are, and I hope it always will be," she adds as a customer who was getting some gasoline says he will be back to pay for it in a few minutes.

About midmorning or a little earlier, a few men gather at the store. They come almost every morning to sit in the rocking chairs in one corner and discuss topics that farmers have discussed for centuries: the weather, politics, the crops, and each other—not necessarily in that order. They share a humor that comes from years of connection to the land and a sense of community.

"One thing about living in the small communities is you get to know everybody and everybody knows you … and your business!" says one gentleman, eliciting laughter and nods of agreement. Then someone mentions the current tobacco crop: "I remember my granddaddy saying that 'Dry weather will scare you to death, but wet weather will starve you.'"

The boundaries between Macedonia and Williamson's Crossroads are ill-defined. Someone says, "It's just past the sharp curve going back toward where Kevin's working." Between the tobacco fields and the store is the center of Williamson's Crossroads, the intersection of Princess Ann Road and Highway 242. There's a Baptist church there and a small café, Country Kitchen. Because of the viral pandemic, some customers get their meals to go, but others come in and sit in the small dining area as Paula Huggins and her helper cook, serve, and collect the money. "Some folks wear masks and others don't," she says, "but we're safe."

Next door, Allen Prevatte has finished mowing his yard and is selling kale to a customer. Not collards. Kale. It's a small garden, so he specializes in a few items.

Tobacco farms, like the ones that Kevin works, are fading from existence. The government bought out the allotment for most of the farmers, and now there are only about ten farms in the whole county still growing and harvesting the crop.

It's been a wet summer for tobacco farmers. Combine that with a hurricane and a couple of tornadoes and thunderstorms, and you wonder why any farmers plant seeds and take their chances year after year.

"It's all I've ever done," is Kevin's answer as to why he continues to toil in the tobacco fields when so many of his neighbors have slipped the bonds of their heritage and turned to more corn and soybeans.

"Oh, tobacco farming has changed a lot," Kevin says. "There's no more auction. We contract with Philip Morris and R.J. Reynolds. It's immediate. As soon as we take it to them, we get paid. The contract gives us a budget guide. But you can't budget for things like we've faced this year. We have a total of fifty-eight acres—thirty-eight acres drowned from all this rain—and we had to go out in the fields and stand up a lot that got blown over by the hurricane. This is the first time in thirty years that we've had drowned tobacco."

He watches the mechanical harvester advance toward him through the field, light-green leaves picked from the stalk then falling into a trailer. The trailer will take the leaves to the curing barns, metal structures that will dry the leaves to a golden brown. There are only two people working at the barn.

"Tobacco farming is not as dependent on manual labor as it used to be, but equipment is expensive," he notes. "We handle tobacco a lot different from the way we used to. My father-in-law taught me everything I know about tobacco. He was my mentor. He taught me how to adapt to change, to the way we sell it and the way we grow and harvest it."

It's probable that Bobby is looking down on Kevin and Donna, whispering heavenly guidance. A farmer growing tobacco needs all the help he can get.

Freeman

"Used to be" is a common phrase heard in Freeman.

"Used to be Pierce Wyche and Co. had a store here, right where Dyno Cam is now. My mama used to go there all the time. You could get just about anything you needed. Lot like the one at Hallsboro. I remember Mr. Paul Wyche used to give her a break on the price on stuff sometimes." These were not words from a single voice but from many who responded when first asked about Freeman.

"Used to be a post office there and the train would stop there," was another phrase often heard. Nobody remembers exactly when that was; "bout 1900 sometime" is the only estimate.

This morning a soft rain is falling, but it doesn't seem to affect the traffic on Highway 74/76. Highway 11 takes the northerly traffic, mostly log trucks headed to the mill at Riegelwood. The folks at the little garage just east of the junction of Money Hole Road and the main highway haven't yet decided to venture out in the gray weather, remaining inside until the decision is made.

But just down the highway, past the usual mélange of houses and mobile homes, Danny Graham and his wife, Yolanda, are getting ready for another day at Livingston Creek Farmers Market, a part of Livingston Creek Farm. (The actual creek runs just a little way farther east of the market.) They put out fresh tomatoes, corn, okra, turnips, butter beans, and cabbage, along with other vegetables. In another little building, they have fresh seafood brought in early this morning or yesterday afternoon from a Brunswick County beach.

The little bit of rain stops abruptly, and the sunshine bursts like a floodlight on the site, giving it an almost festive air. A car pulls into the parking area, and a woman emerges quickly and goes into the covered produce stand. With Yolanda's assistance, the woman buys a few items and is back on the road in just a few minutes.

"Musta wanted something for breakfast," Danny says, with a laugh. Laughter comes easily to Danny. His amiable disposition belies his intimidating appearance. He's about fifty and a mountain of a man, standing way more than six feet tall with the additional height of a pair of black cowboy boots. He's got on a black T-shirt that emphasizes his muscled body and a black cowboy hat to match. A waxed handlebar mustache completes the impression that this man could do you some damage if he decided to.

It doesn't take long to realize that his appearance is just a façade. Underneath that tough image is a man who likes people and likes to talk to people. Soon an open and friendly discourse develops between Danny and a visitor.

When asked why he built his unique business, Danny's answer says much about him. "I always wanted to sell vegetables by the side of the road," he says. "I used to work for a big corporation. Made good money, saved it, and when I thought I was ready, I bought this place. I've done well. Folks around here have been good to me. Met a lot of wonderful people who have become regular customers."

Danny had planned to include a small café where he would serve garden- and sea-to-table meals. "But I couldn't find anybody who wanted to work to help me build it," he explains.

In addition to the produce and seafood sales, Livingston Creek Farms also offers hiking and camping areas for overnight and longer stays. "Had a fellow come the other day and stayed seven days," Danny says. "I believe he loved this place!

"I wanted to build something here. This is home. I like it here. I have ties here," he explains.

When asked what has changed the most here over the years, he replies: "We don't talk to each other as much as we used to. We talk to our cellphones more than we do to each other. It would solve a lot of problems if we just talked more to each other."

That's what Danny does this morning: talk to people. Some he already knows; some he has just met. But before a visitor leaves, he doesn't feel like a visitor anymore. He's now a friend.

It has begun to rain again. This time it builds from the south, and soon a clap of thunder sends everyone under the big produce shelter or to their cars. Those customers who head west are directed around a stalled car at the Highway 11 intersection. The then-northward traffic goes by several acres of cleared woodland owned by the paper company. Looking at all the cutover land, it is optimistic for the traveler to remember that timber is a renewable resource. Trees will grow there again.

Pireway

Seven Creeks Highway and Swamp Fox Highway also are Highway 904/905, respectively. When they come together in the southeastern corner of Columbus County, the intersection could be called Downtown Pireway. Calling it that is not as outrageous as it sounds. There was a time when Pireway was a thriving farming and logging center with a jailhouse, store, and turpentine distillery. Folks floated large rafts of timber down the Waccamaw River from Pireway, North Carolina, to Georgetown, South Carolina. Over the years, there has been a post office designated as Pyraway, and one nineteenth-century map named the city Tar Landing or Pierewan's Ferry. As they do with every swamp in the area, historians claim that Francis Marion, the Swamp Fox himself, took refuge from the Tories here during the Revolutionary War.

Just a little way past the intersection of the two highways where 905 heads north, the Waccamaw River runs quietly under the road. But this morning, unlike in the past, there is no evidence of river commerce. There's a boat landing there, and several trucks with boat trailers are parked in the parking lot. The boatmen have slipped under the branches of the cypress trees in search of fish or just some peace and quiet.

This is the southernmost part of the Waccamaw River in Columbus County. The river continues its winding way from its origin at Lake Waccamaw to Georgetown where, according to some expansive pronouncements, it creates the Atlantic Ocean.

Although the river still plays a major role in the lives of Pireway's residents, the area is primarily farming country. Travelers on the two major highways can see some of the farmers beginning the fall harvest even as the late summer sun pounds its heat on the fields. Combines stir up dust and corn husks as they maneuver down the long rows of the fields that have been soaked by rain and blown and twisted by the wind. This will not be the best year for corn and soybeans, but these folks have persevered through difficult times before and prevailed in the struggle. They'll do it again.

A few miles east of the Highway 904/905 intersection is Fowler's Supermarket. Pete Duncan owned the store before Lawrence Fowler bought it in 1993. Fowler's used to sell some of everything. It still sells a lot of groceries and some clothes. But today the primary drawing card is a custom meat market frequented not only by the local folks but also by the many beachgoers who stop by on a regular basis. It has become almost a tradition, a part of the trip, to stop by Fowler's and get steaks and pork chops to eat with all the seafood to be consumed while at the beach.

And local folks have made it a tradition to come by every morning to get a snack and visit with their neighbors. James Benton comes in looking for company, but there aren't any cronies to chat with this morning. "I'd be just about lost without this store," he says. "Look forward to coming in every morning."

Other folks come in, and in a few minutes, there is a line at the cash register. Going to be a good day.

Benton leaves Fowler's and heads eastward toward the intersection. He turns north on 905, and in a few miles, just before he reaches another swamp crossing, he stops at Roscoe's Country Store. There are a couple of cars parked away from the gas pumps. That means they are probably going to be there for a while.

The store is a simple cinder block construction with a modest sign over the door. Inside, Sheila Singletary sits behind a small counter at a cash register, and Gary Faulk and his brother Kelvin—regular customers—are seated under a window and in front of the counter. James buys a soft drink and joins in the conversation, a ritual he missed this morning at Fowler's. Shortly, Harold and Lacy Gore join them.

Their conversation is wide ranging:

"When the Lord made the Garden of Eden, he patterned it after this part of the earth."

"People in Fair Bluff bring their champion watermelons over here for us."

"Used to be a railroad ran across the river."

"Had a constable one time, full-time right down here."

"Jackson Brothers Lumber Company logged all down in here."

"We are in Nakina, but a lot of folks think Nakina is just up to the school, but that ain't all of it."

"There ain't been a ferry at Reeves Ferry to my knowledge."

"It was a ferry back before the Civil War."

Sheila says: "Been here off and on since April 1st, 1956. Not as busy as we used to be. Seems like everybody nowadays goes to town every day. We don't carry as much here now as we used to either. The wholesalers don't think we sell enough to keep us on their delivery route."

But for folks like Gary and Kelvin and Harold and Lacy and James and the other regulars, there is enough: enough soft drinks, enough snacks, enough watermelon on a hot day, enough boiled peanuts to fill you up, and enough friendship to last a lifetime. That is the kind of thing that ties communities like Pireway and Nakina and even the undefined Dula and Olyphic together—that and the history and the river.

WHITEVILLE

Although the sun is shining, there is a chill in the air this morning. A little mist rises from Soules Swamp as it crosses under South Madison Street in Whiteville. It is an incongruous sight to stand on a swamp bridge and look down the busy main street of a town. But Whiteville is no ordinary town. If a visitor were to "take a mind to," he could walk through the heart of Whiteville north from the swamp bridge to the steps of a majestic courthouse. Along the way, he could see buildings that have been a part of the landscape for many years still standing, still useful, adapting to change and challenges. In those buildings, those homes and businesses, are resilient people, some with deep roots here and some transplants making their own unique contribution to a new history.

Appropriately, the first business heading up Madison Street is Sunshine Laundry and Cleaners, a place where old is made like new again every day, just like the street itself. Within sight of the bridge is The Men's Den, Ronnie Faulk's barber shop that he has operated "for a long time." The barber shop used to be a little hot dog and burger stand, The Circle Drive In. But Ronnie has made his own mark on the place—a place where men and women go to get their hair cut and styled and where Ronnie's expertise and personality make friends out of customers. Ronnie greets each customer by name, goes through the traditional Southern greeting of "How's your mama and them?" and generally creates such a convivial atmosphere that the haircut becomes a secondary consideration. Storm water has flooded his place just about every time there is a heavy rain.

On the corner of the next block is an art center. An art center in a small rural town? Yes. The center encourages creativity with funding and venues to help folks to find expression and beauty even when flood waters and hurricanes and sickness cast a shadow on the area. Art can brighten the darkest night, even when the night is flooded.

Downtown Whiteville literally has something for just about everybody: lots of eateries, from fine dining to very casual, as well as clothing stores, furniture stores, drug stores, etc. Most visitors wouldn't know that those buildings along both sides of Madison Street have been used for more than one purpose now in the process of revitalization. Guiton's Drug Store and the old Moskow's Department Store are undergoing change for the first time in many years.

But change isn't new. Just across the street, Pricilla Hinson is putting up a beautiful Christmas display in the Sugar and Spice store that used to be a movie theater. At the end of the block, the new Lee Lee's at Madison and Main has replaced the iconic Mann's Store that stood there for many years.

Across the railroad track, the old train depot has become an event center for just about any kind of social activity. The depot and downtown have been the center of The Pecan Harvest Festival every November for more than a quarter of a century. Sadly, the pandemic did what hurricanes and floods couldn't do, so the festival was canceled in 2021. But it'll be back.

The old Waccamaw Bank is now Dr. Peggy Barnhill's office. The old Columbus Theater marquee is now an electronic billboard. Just about every business on the street was something else originally.

Jenny Holcomb and Jan McPherson are coming back to their office on the corner of the block. They have probably been visiting some of the businesses this morning to hear what those folks have to say and what they need to help their businesses. Holcomb is executive director of the Columbus County Chamber of Commerce and Tourism and McPherson is the head of the downtown development office. Always smiling and positive, always encouraging that "entrepreneurial spirit," that's what they say keeps this little town going strong even as similar towns give way to modern challenges.

"It's the personality of the community. These folks never give up. They persist when others quit," Holcomb says. "They have this perseverance that says, 'We'll not be defeated by floods or pandemics.'"

"We can beat this," McPherson adds. "So they sweep out the water and mud, work with the city to do something about the drainage, rebuild and repaint, because that's what they do."

Where else could you find new business starting up during a pandemic? As a visitor listens to conversations downtown, he gets the sense that the town is in the middle of a renaissance or, more aptly, a reincarnation—a whole new life based on a legacy of persistence and perseverance.

A hamburger and Coke from the iconic Ward's Grill—or any of the other eateries—will fortify a visitor who wants to tread the Madison Mile, the distance from the railroad track to the courthouse, also known as "from downtown to uptown." The street runs north past a wide variety of businesses: restaurants, auto detailer on one side, and auto retailer on the other. Not many folks know that there was once a busy hotel on that corner where the car lot is. Right across from First Citizens Bank is a building that was once also a bank but is now the North Carolina Museum of Natural Science in Whiteville. It is the most unique science museum. It is only a short walk or shorter drive back to that bridge and a swamp that is a living example of nature's wonders, a place where students can get a firsthand look at what they learn about at the museum. Not many museums can provide that immediate, living classroom.

The town hall stands shining and new on the edge of the residential section of Madison Street, just past Sub-Sational, another downtown eatery. The street becomes pure Americana: houses and churches of all styles and sizes, people walking and jogging past neatly kept lawns. If Norman Rockwell had been a Southerner, he would have painted Madison Street.

About halfway between the railroad and the courthouse, Kenwood Royal turns his house and yard into an annual Christmas showcase, including a red-nosed reindeer on the roof. For many young and old, it's not Christmas until Rudolph's nose starts blinking on top of the Royal house.

Just down the street from the Royal house is the end of the Madison Mile. The stately county courthouse stands there in the middle of a traffic circle, the national, state, and county flags flying at full staff. It's the kind of sight that makes your heart beat a little stronger—maybe even brings a tear to your eye—as you feel a little bit of pride when the late afternoon sun casts its light on the solid red-brick structure with giant white columns.

There are two men sitting on the courthouse steps, looking south down Madison Street. Jim and Jess Hill, father and son respectively, are both attorneys. Both were born and raised in the county, and both have been a part of the justice system for many years. Jim was county attorney for many years and still practices law from his office just across the street from the old courthouse. Jess was a magistrate and is now the clerk of court for the county. Both worked in that old courthouse.

"I remember when all the county's business was in this one building," Jim says. "Everything that affected the life of the people of this county was somehow connected to this building."

"Of course, county operations outgrew the old building, and we now have a new courthouse—but this building is still important. It is our connection not only to the past but can still be functional in the modern age," Jess notes. He has a unique perspective on the old courthouse. Not only did his father serve as county attorney, but his mother-in-law, Celia Pridgen, also served as clerk of court.

A visitor made the analogy that the courthouse was a little like Jim. It may be getting a little older, but it's still a viable and valuable resource. And as Jess and Jim have their unique and personal connection to courthouse history, so do all the people of the county, because every person whose family has lived here, as well as their children and grandchildren, has inherited a legacy that is indelibly connected to that building.

The sun is setting behind the Memory's Store (Bill Gore's law office now) just as it has since the old building was built there just across from the courthouse more than a century ago. Most of the buildings that now compose the "courthouse square" are professional offices where commercial establishments once stood.

Up and down North and South Madison Street is proof that people who care about their town exist in every generation.

Riegelwood/Armour

Fog has settled heavily over Money Hole Road this morning, making travel on the little curvy route from Freeman to Riegelwood more hazardous than usual. Fortunately, traffic is very light—almost nonexistent. There is not much reason to go down this road unless you live here. Nobody seems to know how the road got its name. Not many people even ask.

When it connects with Old Lake Road, a right turn takes the traveler through the community of Armour. Richard Love was the postmaster back in 1876. *Amour* is the French word for "love" so, with a little misspelling, the town got its name.

The most distinctive structure is the Armour school, now Acme-Delco Elementary School. Although the school is no longer operating, the now-empty building is still the most identifiable element in the community.

A little farther down the road is a sign directing travelers to West Frazier sawmill. Although it is in Armour, the address for the mill, like everything else in Armour, is Riegelwood. There were some community problems concerning air quality and the West Frazier mill a while back, but that has now been resolved—somewhat. The sawmill is operating today, but there is no traffic in and out of the site and nothing in the air but clouds.

The Old Lake Road ends at the village of Riegelwood wherein lies the most prominent industry in Columbus County: International

Paper Company. Originally, it was Reigel Paper Corporation. The first appearance was in Bolton, where the woodlands office was located. Those early foresters were assigned the job of making the great Green Swamp an available resource for wood before the paper mill was to be built. Their efforts paid off. Those trucks hauling logs to the mill this morning are still taking logs from the Green Swamp and from miles around because the companies have instituted, kept, and promoted good private forestry practices that enable harvesting and replenishing the raw product they need to make paper without harm to the environment.

Several years ago, Federal Paper bought the plant, then sold it to Reigel Paper Company. Riegelwood, named after the original company, is still a company town. The corporation owns a large portion of the land, but its influence spreads all around the nebulous boundary of the town.

The early morning fog has begun to lift. The company has made significant changes to reduce emissions into the air. There was a time when the fog in the area would be so thick that traffic along the main Highway 87 and Highway 74/76 would almost come to a standstill. Fortunately, that is not the case this morning.

There is an almost steady stream of log trucks going in and out of the mill. The mill creates an industrial skyline in an otherwise rural portrait. It is big, and it dominates the town. A lot of work has gone into making the plant more environmentally friendly: less smoke rises from the smoke stacks, and the old familiar smell is almost gone, even on a foggy morning like this.

The road from the mill goes by the credit union and terminates in what is considered "downtown" Riegelwood. There is a post office, grocery store, doctor's office, and a convenience store gas station here. To guard against the coronavirus, most folks at the grocery store put on and adjust their masks before entering.

The diesel fuel pump behind the station provides ample room for the big trucks to enter and exit the fueling area. A truck drives up and parks in the large parking area that is pocked with several mudholes. The driver exits the truck and walks the hundred or so yards to get his lunch at Subway. It is a lot less trouble than trying to get that big rig closer to the store.

Just as the sun bursts from behind the clouds, Trey Teele pulls up to refill the big tank of his log truck. Teele makes two trips a day from the Farmville/Greenville area to the mill and back—ten hours a day.

"No, not my truck … yet," he responds to a question about ownership of the rig. "But one day. Soon, I hope." It takes a while for him to fill the tanks with diesel fuel, so he sets the nozzle on automatic and goes into the convenience store to get a snack and a soft drink.

Jimmy Allen drives his unloaded truck up to the diesel pump. "Oh yeah," he says, "I been driving a truck up here near 'bout every morning since I got outta high school. My family was in the logging business, and it just seemed natural that I kept doing what they'd been doing," he says, as he puts the gasoline nozzle in the huge gas tank. "I got to go back to the other side of Whiteville to get the other load, then load up this evening and have one ready for in the morning."

The smell of pine resin and mud still clings to the truck and mixes with the smell of the diesel fuel. It is a unique odor, one that is not likely to be found in many places. It's like a signature, an odoriferous logo of a lifestyle that has been a part of this area for many years, a lifestyle of independence shared with the land, with nature.

"We don't make a lotta money, but I like what I do. Take care of my family. Got a daughter going to Campbell this fall. She's worked every summer to save for school, and she got a little scholarship money from a beauty pageant. Don't hurt to be pretty and smart," Jimmy says with a laugh. "And I done pretty good with my logging. Most expensive thing is keeping this truck rolling. Something's always tore up. But it's a good life."

Jimmy leaves the gas pumps and drives out onto Highway 87 back toward Tabor City. He may notice the sign just down the road that says Riegelwood Country Club. Jimmy's probably not going there today, but there is a car headed up the little road toward the club.

The "Country Club" title might be a little misleading. The clubhouse is a small cinder block building set among some pine trees with a golf course in the background. It is a community course, a part of Riegelwood that John L. Reigel had built when the plant was built. He didn't want to have to go to Wilmington to play. Now the community keeps up the nine-hole course. It's got a new manager, though he isn't here today. There are no golfers on the course, but the guy in the office says folks will show up later, some to play and some to help take care of the grounds. This is a real community country club.

Back up on the highway going east is a park with a baseball field and a soccer field. People are mowing their lawns and trimming shrubbery at churches, and there is a young woman pushing a baby in a stroller down a street by the baseball field. The fog is completely gone now, and the sun is bearing down. The young woman and her baby get into a car parked near the ballfield—the car a haven complete with air conditioning in a company town with happy people.

Acme-Delco

Folks looking for lunch in Delco have to do a little foraging in light of the pandemic. The little drive-through hot dog stand is closed, and the Highway 55 café is providing only takeout as is the fairly new restaurant out on the highway just before it enters Brunswick County. That may be where Parks Thomas bought his lunch today. He is eating in his office in the back of the drugstore he operates.

Parks is a native of Columbus County and came back home to practice his profession after graduating from the University of North Carolina at Chapel Hill. He lived and worked at Lake Waccamaw and Elizabethtown, where he still lives, then had a drugstore in the village of Riegelwood for several years. Then, a few years ago, he moved to the little shopping center on the highway in Delco and opened his current store still called Riegelwood Mutual Drug.

"I like being an independent pharmacist in an area like Delco. I get to know my customers, and that allows us to better serve them. I know the medical needs of some of my customers so well that I can usually tell if a medicine they are wanting will interact favorably or unfavorably with medicine they are currently taking. Sometimes I can remember that without looking it up. Saves them and us a lot of grief sometimes," he says.

On this particular day, Parks is less likely to personally see each customer. His assistants are busy taking prescriptions at the drive-through window due to coronavirus restrictions. "The virus does keep me from personally greeting and talking to my customers. Because I've been here and in Riegelwood so long, I made a lot of friends here. That's one reason I stay in business here and drive back and forth to Elizabethtown every day. It's like I have two homes." Parks's conversation is interrupted by a request by one of his assistants to sign a form. "I plan to stay here a while longer. I'm a young old man," he says and laughs.

Ronald McPherson's store, McPherson Hardware, sits at the intersection of Cronly Drive and Highway 87, the unofficial, loosely defined center of what is referred to by the locals as "Acme-Delco." Cronly is just one of many names this community has had over the years. The post office in 1835 was called Robinson's after the postmaster at the time, then, when the railroad came through, was changed to Brinkley. The newscaster David Brinkley claimed his family moved from here to Wilmington. About the turn of the century, Hugh McCrae, who founded several such "colonies," enticed immigrants from Hungary, Poland, and Germany to settle here, and they changed the name to New Berlin. Then when World War I came along, the name was changed to Pershing, in honor of the general. But somehow mispronunciation changed it to Perishing. Community residents didn't like that designation, so they wanted to change it.

"There are several stories of where the name came from," Ronald says. "One was that Mr. L.R. Hobbs, the postmaster, had installed a Delco lighting system powered by a Delco generator. Besides the post office, the generator provided light for the school. He decided to call the community Delco.

"Further on down, Livingston Creek was another little community whose postmaster was named Cronly. When Acme Manufacturing built a plant there about 1900, they changed the name to Acme. So now you got Acme-Delco. You can pick whatever story you want." Appropriately, Cronly Street runs through Delco to Acme.

Ronald's store is not the first on Cronly Street to sell hardware and farm supplies. The Old Acme Store, which opened back in the 1920s, is at the north end of Cronly Street in Acme. Some folks say that the original store was built by the same folks that got Pierce and Company in Hallsboro and Pierce-Wyche at Freeman. Like so much of the history of Acme-Delco, much of it is speculation.

"'Bout all we can do is speculate. And when you and me and our generation is gone, there won't even be any guesswork 'cause won't nobody care," Ronald says to this visitor.

Ronald's son, Ron Jr., works with his father in the store. He attends to customers as Ronald continues his conversation with the visitor. He is helping a man and woman for whom English is a second language, so much of the conversation is subject to frequent breaks for interpretation.

Ronald is in a philosophical mood this afternoon: "I miss the old days when everybody knew each other. Not that we don't have a lot of good folks living around here now, but it's a different feeling. People come in here with their head crooked sideways, holding a phone on their shoulder. They'll find what they want, pay for it, and never say a word except to whoever is on the phone. Folks used to come in here, and we'd talk awhile, drink a Co'Cola, and eat a pack o' Nabs."

As if to confirm Ronald's assertion, a customer comes in and buys a piece of hardware and unknowingly pays for the visitor's soft drink that was sitting beside the cash register. "That was nice of him," Ronald laughs.

"Still a lot of good people around," he continues. "Some just more involved with their neighbors than others. You wouldn't worry about what people say about you if you knew how little they thought about you."

The day is winding down in Acme-Delco as Ronald and Ron close up the store. Just down the road a mile or two back toward Freeman, Christy Malpass is cutting the hair of her last customer for the day. Her little shop is considerably off the main road, and because of the coronavirus, she has to limit occupation to one customer at a time. "Before this virus stuff, there would be a lot of conversation going on in here. I love my customers. I don't just fix their hair; I think of them as friends," she says as the electric clippers clear off much of the customer's hair that has grown beyond its normal length since the state forced the closing of beauty salons and barber shops.

Much of Christy's conversation is about her family: her husband, her children, and grandchildren. Christy looks way too young to be a grandmother.

"This is where I put my shop, because this is where I live. Not in the shop," she laughs, "but here in Delco. This is where my husband is from, so this is my home. I like being home. I like being a part of the community and knowing my customers. I like the community. We've got good schools and a lot of churches and hardworking people. We care about each other, and God provides well for us." That's a good attitude to have at the end of the day in Delco or anywhere.

CERRO GORDO

Winter has come to Cerro Gordo, at least for today. A soft wind blows the misty rain even as a small group of folks stand outside the Valero convenience store/service station. The current concern about the COVID-19 pandemic is stronger than the weather for those regulars who come each morning to get their coffee and incidental breakfast. But as the mist turns to drizzle then to rain, they reluctantly get in their cars and head out for the rest of the day.

Some habits are hard to break, and gathering at the store has been a routine for folks for many years. Adele Shamake bought the store just a few months ago. Even during the pandemic, he had faith in the community, and that confidence has paid off.

"I'm glad I came to Cerro Gordo," he says. "These are good people here, and they have supported my store despite all the uncertainty." He bought the store in the summer, not knowing whether West Columbus High School across the road would be open in the fall.

Even as the early-morning customers are leaving, others are pulling up to the gas pumps or going into the store. There is a four-way stop on Highway 76 between the station and the school. This morning there seems to be some confusion on the part of drivers headed east and west. One car approached the intersection from the west and slid through the crossing as he applied the brakes—too late to stop before the sign. It could have been because the rain blurred his vision of the sign and the blinking red light, or he might have been a longtime resident still getting used to the new signs.

There are several cars parked in the parking lot of the high school and the elementary school just down the road. Jeff Greene, the principal of the high school, is at the school today, as are most of the teachers. The students are learning from home via the internet.

"We've had to make some adjustments," Greene says. "But overall, we're making the best of a bad situation." He notes that the current enrollment is down, but that the situation is not all related to the pandemic.

"Some of that decline is due to families that moved as a result of all the flooding in the past few years, and young families that would otherwise be sending children to school here have gone elsewhere to find work," he says.

The high school is newer than the elementary school, but both facilities play a vital role in the community. Part of the old school will be torn down to make room for a new elementary school that will encompass the current schools in Fair Bluff and Evergreen as well as Cerro Gordo.

But the schools aren't the only things adding to the growth of the little town. Although Cerro Gordo is the smallest municipality in the county, it is experiencing a lot of growth. There is a new Family Dollar store on the northwest corner of the intersection. Due to recent flooding, it is the only place in the county to buy groceries west of Chadbourn. It may not be a supermarket, but it beats a drive of several miles to get a loaf of bread.

Two customers at Family Dollar have secured their purchases in their cars and are standing in the rain under one umbrella. Whether it is a serious discussion or a "How's-your-mama-and-them?" exchange, it's the type of thing that only happens in small communities where conversation between neighbors overrules the weather.

Right beside the Family Dollar store is G&G Healthcare. It houses the offices of Dr. Melvin Gerald and Elvington Drugs. The drugstore had been on Main Street in Fair Bluff for many years until successive floods made the move necessary. G&G Healthcare is owned by three brothers, Melvin, Paul and Keith, who grew up in Cerro Gordo and came back home to create a general medical practice to provide medical service to "whoever needs it."

Another kind of medical service is available just across from the G&G offices. This one provides medical care for all kinds of animals: large animals (cows, horses, hogs, llamas, etc.) as well as cats and dogs and an occasional rabbit or chicken. Dr. Jeff Burroughs brought his practice to Cerro Gordo from Wake County partly because "There were enough veterinarians in Wake County." Plus, this is the home of his wife, Tiffany.

The waiting room has two feline patients waiting patiently while two dog owners keep their canine charges outside. In any other year, the sight of so many people wearing masks at the vet's office would indicate a large staff. But the pandemic has made such a sight not unusual nowadays; everybody wears a mask.

Probably the most unique business in Cerro Gordo is the Black's Tire Racing Team—longtime residents of the town and owners of Black's Tire and Auto Service, which sponsors the racing team and has offices in several states. It's surprising to most people who are aware of stock car racing, one of the most popular sports in the country, that a little town like Cerro Gordo could spawn a NASCAR-level participant who not only "ran with the big boys" but placed thirteenth in the prestigious Daytona 500—the first time it ran in the race! Usually the racing shop would be buzzing with preparation for the next race, but, like all professional sports, the pandemic has taken its toll, and everyone is waiting for the opportunity to get back on the track.

On the southeastern edge of town is the new town hall. Mayor David White and the other town leaders secured the assistance of the Golden Leaf Foundation in obtaining the grant to provide funding for the building. When a visitor notes the apparent growth of the town in the middle of all the travails when other towns seem to be struggling, the mayor says, "We have been blessed. Our economy is prospering, we're getting a new school, and the future looks bright. It is because we have people who care about their community through the good and bad times. We never give up."

That determination began, like almost all the other communities in Columbus County, with the lumber industry. The economic focus changed with the times, but Cerro Gordo still thrives. The history of the town is documented by the people who live there, those whose ancestry is connected to the town for centuries and those who decided to find a new home there.

Cerro Gordo means "fat hill" in Spanish. It was also the name of a battle fought during the Spanish American War. An early resident had a connection to the Battle of Cerro Gordo and decided that the name suited the town. Cerro Gordo sits on a hill, but in this flat country, *hill* is a relative term.

The clouds and rain continue as night falls on the little town. And when the sun comes out tomorrow, it will warm the ground, and the seeds of prosperity will sprout and continue to produce a future to match its past on the fat hill.

CHADBOURN

The railroad tracks cross Brown Street to form the nebulous center of Chadbourn. On a cold midwinter morning, the sun struggles to pierce the gray sky. The rays sift through the dark clouds and settle on the red caboose and the engine sitting next to the R.J. Corman Railroad Company station. Just a little south of the station, trucks are being loaded at Bailey Produce.

Traffic on Brown Street is almost nonexistent. But soon the number of cars will increase as folks heading to the beach make their way south. By midafternoon there will be a steady stream of folks in every manner of conveyance passing through the center of the small town. Some will stop for gas or a quick meal. Some will stop to check out Donna Spivey's musical instruments just a short distance from the railroad tracks. But most people will slow down only because of the stoplights.

Just down from the intersection on Railroad Street, Myles Cartrette is getting ready for another day of restoring the old Lewis house. For many years, the big Georgian-style residence was the showplace of the town. Then time and storms took their toll, and it lay in ruins until Myles, "under God's direction," decided to restore it.

"Restoration is the theme: restore this old home and use it to restore the lives of ministers who need solace, encouragement, and restoration." That's what Myles says he came back home to do. With the continued help of many people and the determination of a man who says God is leading him, the task will be completed. The future is building on the past.

The sun is slowly creeping westward back toward the intersection. It lights up McArthur Supply Inc. Although the company is under new ownership, it opens just as it has since 1907. Steady. Permanent. Constant. Things that reflect the stability of a town that has faced and is continuing to face the challenges of change.

Some things like Debbie McKeithan's beauty shop never change. She might modernize it a little bit, but the same ladies will come to get their hair done in the little shop downtown. Debbie bought the shop from Raymond Bass when it was a barber shop. Judy, one of her regular customers, comes from Whiteville. Soles works part-time with Miss Debbie. The activity and conversation this morning look like a scene from *Steel Magnolias*. Ladies can get a permanent here because Debbie's not going anywhere. "I'm still making a living here," she declares.

There's another beauty shop just a couple of blocks north of Debbie's on Brown Street. It's called The Pretty Parlor, and Marieka Cooper, Shenika Shipman, and Jasmine Thompson are "fixin' up" some folks this morning. Jasmine's baby girl, Zariah, gets her hair done by her mama. This is a new business; it's only been open since October 2020, but it already is a busy place.

"We're open every day, but because of COVID, we haven't been able to lately," Marieka says. She's a Chadbourn native who went down to Atlanta and returned home because, she says, "My town needed me."

Another former resident came back home to make a difference too. Greg Thompson bought the building on the corner of Brown Street between Debbie's and Mariana's shops. Although Greg's permanent home still is in Orlando, Florida, he makes frequent trips back home to Brown Street Station, bringing a variety of shows and events—musical concerts, comedians, variety acts, and tribute performers—to what once was a feed store.

"Home is where the heart is," Greg says. "Chadbourn is home, and when I saw what was happening in other small towns around the country, I wanted to do something like that for Chadbourn. So, at the suggestion of Lisa Blake, I bought the old Dixie Farm Supply and turned it into a performance and event venue. I have met many folks who are small-town investors. Every one of them has told me that investing in small towns is the wave of the future. I want to be a part of making things happen in my hometown. And things will happen! I believe Chadbourn can rely on its history to build the future, and the future is bright!"

The noon sun now is directly overhead, and Cindy's Kountry Kitchen is full of lunch-time customers. Like every business during the COVID crisis, Cindy's has seen a decline in business. But now there are folks hungry for breakfast and lunch and each other's company, so they come to Cindy's to eat and find out how their neighbors are doing. During all the eating, there is a group on the side of the room taking up a collection for a family whose house recently burned. That's the kind of thing people do in Chadbourn.

Densil Worthington is at the funeral home preparing for a service. He is the owner of Worthington Funeral Home and has been extra busy lately with all the COVID deaths. Although death is a part of Densil's life, he is not immune to the sadness.

"Yes, I still feel a sadness when we have a funeral for a friend of mine, for people I've known all my life. The frequency of death doesn't make it less significant to me," he says.

Because his family has deep roots in Chadbourn, Densil is able to look at the past and the future of the town from a unique perspective.

"You know, much of our settlement was due to immigrants, the Sunny South Colony that responded to advertisements for an opportunity to come here and build the future for their families. I think we're on the brink of a new 'immigration,'" he says.

"When a house goes on the market in Chadbourn, it sells in a few days," he adds. "Our proximity to the beaches appeals to people who like the small-town advantages mixed with the availability of the beach, and Wilmington, and the educational opportunities of the University of North Carolina at Wilmington, and the University of North Carolina at Pembroke, as well as Southeastern Community College."

Densil had not intended to go into the family business. He went off to East Carolina University, got his degree, tried other jobs, but came back home because "The family needed me. And this is home. That's a unique asset for any business. You know the people you deal with because they are just like you. We share the same history and the same hopes and dreams. And when the new folks settle here, they become a part of that," he says.

The dark clouds that have hung on all day finally have begun to drop some precipitation. Even as the rain begins to fall, two boys ride their bicycles by the funeral home and then turn toward the downtown area, enjoying life even in the rain.

On the other side of town, Perry Frink is preparing for the Sunday services at the First Missionary Baptist Church, where he is associate pastor. The sturdy brick structure sits on a quiet street among small houses and neatly kept lawns. Perry grew up in Chadbourn, graduated from the local schools, and went to Southeastern Community College, where he was not only a student in the audiovisual technology area but became almost a part of the college himself because he met many people who came for interviews at the campus television studio.

"Sue Hawks was my mentor and friend," Perry says. She, along with Perry's mother, father, and grandfather, taught him the value of work, faith, and perseverance. He earned his degree from Southeastern Community College and his bachelor's degree from Fayetteville State (he drove back and forth every day from Chadbourn), got his master's degree, taught at Johnston Community College (drove back and forth every day), and then finally came back to be the digital support specialist for Truist Bank. Now he's the man who solves all the computer problems that arise.

To every current and former resident of Chadbourn, the Strawberry Festival is a big deal. Perry remembers the exhilaration of the parade, the rides—and all the strawberries he could eat. "I had a great childhood in Chadbourn. I wouldn't change a thing," he says.

So, like all the other people on this day in Chadbourn, Perry came home. (Actually, he never left.) And he decided he wanted to help make the town not like it was, but better. He is active in youth sports, church, and the recently organized Revitalization Committee that brings all the races together for a common purpose in a town with a tremendously diverse population.

Lisa Blake is at the railroad depot museum getting things ready for one of the many events held there. Lisa is kind of a "town activist," constantly looking for ways to make the community attractive to both current and prospective residents. "I love history, and I grew up here, and Chadbourn is like family," she says. "I want to preserve that history and celebrate it." Toward that end, she has helped organize the Turnaround Downtown Revitalization Committee. She wants to preserve, restore, and repurpose the buildings that are so much a part of the heritage of Chadbourn. A grant from Campbell University will fund the establishment of a park at the middle school, one means of bolstering that sense of community. The town of Chadbourn could share the motto of Campbell University: *Ad astra per aspera*," which translates to "To the stars through difficulty." They have experienced an exodus of young people, like so many small towns, and the once-burgeoning tobacco culture has almost disappeared.

When asked, "Why are you here?" every answer on this day was "This is where my heart is. This is home." That connection fuels a light that can't be extinguished by the challenges that face the little town.

As night falls on Chadbourn, the visitor closes the day by walking back down Brown Street. The streetlights and the automobile headlights mingle with the raindrops, creating a thousand little diamonds dancing on the wet pavement. At the stoplight at the corner of Brown Street Station, cars stop; some folks roll the windows down so they can hear the music coming from Donna's Sunny South Colony Music on one side and Brown Street Station on the other. One is playing "This Little Light of Mine," and the other: "When You Wish Upon a Star." Very appropriate anthems for Chadbourn.

LAKE WACCAMAW AND THE GREEN SWAMP

The morning sun rises up in the Green Swamp and slowly climbs a little higher as the rays ease through the clouds and seep across Lake Waccamaw to the mouth of the Waccamaw River. The dam across the mouth of the river doesn't hinder the sun's movement and only channels the water from the lake as it rushes across the concrete barrier into the river and meanders its way down to Georgetown and the Atlantic Ocean.

It is a sequence of events that has happened in much the same way for thousands of years. Even scientists can't be certain how the lake was formed. Some say a glacier receded, leaving a giant pool of water; some say a shower of meteors struck the Earth, creating pockmarks into which water flowed; others say natural springs created the lake. But the Waccamaw Sioux, the Old People, the early Indian settlers, say that a young brave betrayed a beautiful princess. Around the lake was a great mound of flowers, which she adored and for which she wept a lake to keep the flowers living forever. One of the scientific explanations is probably true, but folks around Lake Waccamaw would rather tell the princess story—with their own variations.

The fall weather this morning is a welcome change from the heat of the summer. Lake Waccamaw provides a respite from the enveloping humidity and high temperature for hundreds of folks—visitors and permanent residents alike—every year during the summer. But today, the summer folks have gone back to their other homes, and the permanent residents are left to enjoy the treasure they cherish all year.

A light mist begins to rise as the sun warms the lake. A soft breeze blows from the south, causing the water to ripple under the many piers jutting out from the homes along the west side of the lake, the side where the canal separates the homes built on the spoil created when the canal was dug from the swamp.

Then the waves softly touch the bluff side of the lake where the ground rises high above the waterline. Lake Shore Drive heads east along the bluff as it rises behind Dale's Seafood. This morning the street hosts early morning walkers as well as several golf carts moving slowly so as to savor the scenery.

North of Lake Shore Drive, up Flemington Drive and on Highway 218 (Andrew Jackson Highway), is the main business center of Lake Waccamaw. Waccamaw Plaza is a small shopping center that provides a gas station, restaurants, a grocery store, a drugstore, and other shops— everything a little town needs. Like the lake itself, the shopping center is quiet but busy, a commercial site in the middle of a natural wonder.

Karen Gore opens up the Lake Waccamaw Depot Museum on Flemington Drive. She is the curator and has been in charge of the place for many years. The old train depot is a showplace, a museum that houses history and artifacts of the train era that is so much a part of the town, and is also a repository for the history of Lake Waccamaw, its environs, and particularly, the recollections of and about the people who have lived here and made their unique contributions.

After Karen enters the museum, she immediately begins setting up for one of the many gatherings of townspeople who view the museum much as a community center. There are guitar jam sessions, card games, and weekly potluck suppers that not only provide income and activity but also a source of fellowship that is distinctive to Lake Waccamaw.

When asked what keeps folks here through the winter, Karen replies, "There's a unique sense of peacefulness here all year, but it is amplified (if you can amplify peacefulness) after the summer folks have gone. There is a calmness that envelopes you. It's almost like a cleansing. But it's not lonely. The lake will keep you company when nobody else can."

On many afternoons, Karen takes advantage of her access to the lake—much as the visitors do. She mounts her bicycle and leaves the depot for a ride along Lake Shore Drive.

Across the road from the depot is the local branch of Boys and Girls Homes of North Carolina, with its campus and farm stretched toward the setting sun. The home is built on land originally owned by a family that brought the thriving lumber and shingle-making business to the area more than a century ago.

Karen turns her bike toward the lake, passes the town hall and fire department and the library, and then heads down Lake Shore Drive. Before her, the lake water sparkles in the late afternoon sun; a few clouds are mixed with a bright whiteness edged with a gray border. "It may rain," Karen says with a laugh. "I don't care. It's part of the cleansing."

The houses are all on the north side of the drive. There are some large majestic homes, some smaller cottages. Some are residences for the summer, but most of the houses on this side of the lake are for year-round residents.

She rides by The Anchorage, once a nightclub, then a home for alcoholics, and now a camp for children. Just a short way past The Anchorage is another camp, the Ambassador Camp. Both places now are quiet after a busy summer of campers.

She rides on down the lake border past the Methodist church, her mind freed of the stress of the day. Shortly, she will come to a sharp turn that will take her on around to Lake Waccamaw State Park. But just before she makes that turn, she stops to talk with a group that gathers almost every evening on the bluff across the road from Eddie Pierce's house.

Karen notes that, as always, Eddie is set up for company; chairs and tables sit awaiting anybody who wants to stop and talk a spell. So she does. At that little stop exists the kind of camaraderie to be found among people who have a lot in common despite their individuality. They all love the lake.

They talk of fishing, the coming local election, fishing, the growing abundance of alligators, and fishing. Karen shares a conversation she had with a couple who were looking for "a quiet place where they would feel safe walking at night." She tells them, "We have that at Lake Waccamaw, but you might want to take a flashlight with you to look out for the alligators." The group sees the humor and reality.

After more conversation than she had planned, Karen realizes that she has "stayed too long at the fair" and must return to the depot before dark. She wanted to be able to ride through the Bella Coola neighborhood, cross Big Creek, and past all those houses all the way to the state park at the other end of the lake. Too bad. She'll miss the sight of the sun setting over the river mouth, where the water still runs over the dam, the river runs down to the sea, fish elude the fishermen, and boats rest quietly in their berths.

But she won't return to the depot alone. Remember, the lake will keep you company when nobody else will.

(Listen to Bill recite this poem, track number 3 on Just Down the Road.*)*

The Green Swamp Diner

The Green Swamp Diner used to be a store,
'til they pulled up the gas tank
and widened the doors.

The sun comes up 'cross the Green Swamp each morn,
a new day a-bornin' 'cause the old one is worn.
Sun shines through the windows over tables and chairs;
folks come in for breakfast in singles and pairs.
They don't come just to eat; they come to share news
of neighbors and needs and a wide variety of views
on politics and government, any subject they choose.
If you listen close to the news that they share
you'll find that the truth is there ... but it's rare.

They talk about logging and farming and such,
how life is hard and the money's not much.
They'll talk 'bout the fish they caught,
'bout that new gun that they bought,
'bout giant deer racks and big bear tracks,
how they trudged through the swamp with a deer on their back.

And somewhere 'tween the grits and bacon
they'll recall all the chances they've taken—
when log chains broke and barns caught fire,
those years when the crops had no buyer,
times God held 'em in the palm of His hand
as bombs burst 'round 'em in a foreign land.

Now, their faces are tired and their hair has turned gray,
and their memory's sometimes a shadow, they say.
The past can shed memory, but there's nothing finer
than starting the day at the Green Swamp Diner.

Civic Clubs Still Serving the Communities

There is a tradition in small Southern towns of neighbors helping neighbors. This is especially evident in times of disaster, but it's more than just a response to an immediate need. Helping meet the continuing needs of the community has become a goal of civic or service clubs. They are constant elements in the tradition of community life that bring individuals together for the benefit of all.

People with common interests have always come together to enjoy the fellowship and discuss those items of mutual interest. Book clubs and sewing circles, garden clubs and church organizations are some of the oldest. But in the twentieth century, there was a boom in the number of voluntary organizations that began to represent the civic consciousness of their communities. They may have had different missions and aims, but they shared a commitment to community service.

Such organizations really blossomed in Columbus County and other areas throughout the South after World War II. One theory as to why there was an increased interest in community service was that the men who had returned home from military service wanted to find a way to make the community they had fought for an even better place to live. Winning the war had been a collective effort, so they thought that same collective effort would be a more effective way to serve and help build their community than what they could accomplish individually.

Most of those groups were part of a national organization, and the clubs had adopted the national goals, as well as addressing the needs of the local community. In addition to other projects, the clubs in North Carolina adopted Boys and Girls Homes of Lake Waccamaw as a project. One of the earliest such clubs was the Tabor City Civitan Club, established in 1939 even before the war was over. Other Civitan clubs were formed in Whiteville in 1946 and another in Hallsboro in 1947. One of the Whiteville club's most popular projects is their pancake suppers. John Gayle Barkley, a longtime member of Civitan, says, "I've enjoyed being a part of Civitan because I enjoyed the fellowship and the satisfaction of doing something for my neighbors and organizations like Boys and Girls Homes."

Fair Bluff, Chadbourn, Tabor City, and Whiteville formed Rotary Clubs. In addition to other projects, the Rotary clubs distributed dictionaries to all third graders in the county and awarded college scholarships.

There were Lions clubs in Fair Bluff in 1966: Chadbourn, Tabor City, Whiteville, and Lake Waccamaw. Their primary goal was to provide assistance to the visually impaired. One of the most popular projects of the Whiteville Lions Club was the annual Merchants and Farmers Exposition. The very popular project brought tremendous crowds to see the exhibits and meet interesting speakers and performers. Stuart Link, the current treasurer of the Lake Waccamaw Club, says, "Being a Lion gives us a chance to give back to our community and to enjoy the camaraderie of doing something together."

In the 1970s, there were Jaycee chapters in Buckhead, Chadbourn, Lake Waccamaw, Tabor City, and Whiteville. The Jaycee organization's primary effort was leadership development. The membership was limited to those under thirty-five years old but later raised to forty. For many years, the Tabor City Jaycees sponsored the Miss Columbus County Pageant. Sometime in the 1970s, the other chapters joined in that project and sent a representative to the Miss North Carolina Pageant each year. The Whiteville Jaycees founded the first rescue squad. Vann Underwood is a past president of the Whiteville Jaycees. Like other civic club leaders, he says, "I enjoyed working on projects as a team. Some of my greatest friendships are my fellow Jaycee members. We were all young men who found a common cause: helping our community. I wouldn't take anything for my Jaycee years."

Whiteville formed an Optimist Club in 1969, and a Kiwanis club followed in 1991. The Optimists Club established a youth baseball program that was and is extremely popular. Its primary emphasis was on youth development. Past president Don Harritan says, "We wanted to provide not just recreation for young people but to show them how to accomplish things together, to learn sportsmanship, and hopefully, they would follow our example of community involvement as they got older."

These clubs were an integral part of the community. Some businesses thought them important enough to pay the membership dues for employees to join a club. It was a part of their job to be involved in the community.

Originally, these clubs were limited to male membership. But as cultural changes came, the clubs adapted to include female members.

The Whiteville Chapter of the North Carolina Federation of Women's Clubs was formed, as well as a Junior Women's Club and Juniorettes. The Woman's Club's official name now is the Whiteville Woman's Civic League. The Lake Waccamaw Woman's Club is not affiliated with the state organization.

Rosanna Ezzell, the current president of the Civic League, points out the organization's broad involvement in education, arts and culture, civic engagement, and public service. She adds that, "We enjoy doing this as a group, and that is part of the satisfaction we get from our involvement."

The organizational structure of the clubs is like that of any other nonprofit organization, which includes a president, vice president, secretary, treasurer, and board of directors. There are other offices related to specific organizations. Holding a local office in any civic club was, and is, a prestigious achievement. Many local members became involved in district, state, and national leadership roles.

In recent years, the number of civic clubs and the number of club members has decreased. There are no longer any Jaycee chapters in the county. Lake Waccamaw and Chadbourn are the only Lions clubs, and there is just one Civitan club in Whiteville. There are Rotary clubs in Whiteville and Fair Bluff, and one Optimist club in Whiteville. Most of the members are seniors. It seems that the younger generation, particularly millennials, choose to participate in community development in a more singular role. According to the *Chronicle of Philanthropy*, a publication that tracks nonprofit giving in the United States, the younger generation still is charitable but chooses to give singularly rather than collectively.

Most clubs have sponsored youth auxiliaries such as Leo clubs with the Lions, Key clubs with Kiwanis, and Interact and Youth Exchange with Rotary. But that is not enough to generate a significant number of younger members to join the parent organization. The Whiteville Optimist has created a separate group called the Wolfpack Optimist, which is primarily concerned with the youth baseball program that has traditionally been a big part of Optimist activity.

Traditions die hard in small Southern towns. There are still festivals celebrating elements of the community that have diminished or disappeared. But the celebration goes on. Civic clubs go on, still dedicated to making a difference in their respective communities even as their membership declines. The two traditions often are joint efforts with the clubs sponsoring and/or participating in the festivals and celebrations. Some civic leaders ascribe this continuation of tradition to civic pride, an attitude of perseverance that has borne them through past difficulties while looking at the positive elements that will propel them to future growth.

Most civic club leaders see the continuation of civic clubs as a challenge. Cultural changes necessitate changes in the service organizations. Some have adapted a technological approach that involves video conferencing where computers bring the members together in a virtual meeting. Others have designated some members as "project members only" who work on club projects but don't attend regular meetings. One local civic club leader predicted that civic clubs would continue as long as there is a need and as long as the community members accept the challenge of meeting those needs.

PART 2
YOUR PEOPLE ARE WHO YOU ARE

Now, Who Was Your Granddaddy?

Genealogy is usually thought of as an activity that provides for an accounting of our ancestors, a history of our family, a tracing of our heritage. At least, that's the theoretical definition. In reality, there are some folks who take a different view.

Some folks make up a lot of their heritage as they go along. It's always amazing to me to listen to some folks expound on their family history from one occasion to another. Here in North Carolina, it's not uncommon to find families whose Scottish heritage takes on the trappings of royalty, depicting every clan as directly descended from Bonnie Prince Charlie himself. Surely, there must have been more of the "common people," or else the Prince was an extraordinarily busy and prepotent sire.

Other folks claim high-ranking descendants from various European families, African chieftains, and Asian princes. Ironically, these same people say we should have stricter immigration laws.

Some folks get deathly serious about their ancestors. They search graveyards (cemeteries to polite folks), looking for names or dates that tell who begat whom and when they did it. Really kinda private stuff to be writing down for people who might not even be family to read about.

Genealogical searches, however, usually are done by a member of the family being researched. In my family, that person was an unmarried female cousin. Appropriately, Cousin Helen was a librarian not unaccustomed to looking through indices of names and familiar with the methodology of research.

These seekers of pedigree can be found in the register of deeds office, in the newspaper archives, and recently and predominately, on the internet. They are looking for anything that might shed some light on the family's past accomplishments and failures, some indication that they might have risen from poverty to prominence or fallen from distinction to anonymity. Of course, the real historian is the one who records everything, the good and the bad, without trying to make the family something it isn't. Cousin Helen was a real historian who told the truth, good and bad.

Some of us might look for ancestors who established the family as "prominent" leaders in the community, while others of us might be more interested in finding out who were the wastrels and brigands—the colorful characters who are far more fascinating.

In any case, the pursuit of family history, while not limited to Southern families, is certainly of concern to almost everyone in the region. And it's not just the "high society" folks who are interested. The activity crosses every boundary of race, religion, and social strata. We all want to know who we were so we might be more likely to know who we are.

We can't choose our relatives, and that's just as well. They probably wouldn't have chosen us anyway. While we all are interested in where we came from, we should remember that the man who boasts only of his roots is conceding that he belongs to a family that's better dead than alive.

REMEMBER WHO YOU ARE

When I was growing up in Hallsboro, Mama often told me, "Remember who you are and where you came from." I don't know why she thought that I could possibly forget, because home becomes a part of us that we can't ever leave. We may travel to far-off places, even live somewhere else for a long time, but we can never leave home. Alfred, Lord Tennyson said we are a part of all that we have met, so we carry those people, places, and events with us no matter where we go.

When I was in college and decided I was going to be an English major and become a writer, I received that old instruction from teachers to "write about what you know." Well, I knew home, so that is what I wrote about. That is what I still write about.

I don't think Mama was worried that I would forget growing up in Hallsboro, Columbus County, North Carolina, the United States of America; I think she might have been concerned that I would see other places that I thought were "better" places than my little hometown. "Better" is a relative term. In what way is one place better than another? It all depends on what you value most.

Several years ago, I wrote an article for a magazine that read, "A small town is a place where people care about you whether you want them to or not." That, to me, is an attribute, a value that means a lot in determining if one place to live is better than another. I want to live where people care about each other, and I want to write about those people so current and succeeding generations will know that the people in small towns and rural communities are important. Not all the important things that happen take place somewhere else.

And that brings me to the importance of community newspapers. My first contact with journalism was with the *News Reporter* when I was in high school. I was a stringer for sports editor Jiggs Powers. I had the menial task of calling in statistics of Hallsboro High School ball games. It was a menial task in relation to the effort of getting the sports story out, and the relative importance of that information was less important than, say, the gubernatorial election. But if I sent in the wrong numbers for a particular player, Jiggs would get a phone call and a chastisement from the parent and/or the coach, and he would pass on that chastisement to me. It was all about accountability of his report, and they had the opportunity to call him or tell him at the next ball game that he was wrong and should correct it. That is what separates community journalism from all other forms of news reporting: the community newspaper is accountable to its readers. Unlike social media or online news sources, readers can challenge the local newspapers.

The community newspaper is not just recording events; it is a part of the community and assumes responsibility for storing the news. Today's current event is tomorrow's history.

We don't have a county museum in Columbus County; we do have some depot museums that do a great job in their respective communities. But if you want to know about the people who live and have lived here and events that happened here, the best place to find that information is in the archives of the *News Reporter*. That's why, at my advanced age, I want to write for my hometown paper. I want to tell the stories of the people, places, and events that make up who we are so that people years from now will know who we were.

Over the years, I have found that there are no ordinary people. Every person has a story that is somehow unique. When I was in the television business, I sought out those people for stories. Some of my television journalist colleagues called them "fluff pieces" because they weren't hard news. But behind every hard news story, there are individuals who made that story happen. It may be a relative or a neighbor, but nobody exists alone. If they do, that in and of itself is a story.

Here in the rural South, we often refer to "our people." That is usually a reference to family, to kin, to relatives. My people are all the individuals that I meet and have met. And I want to tell their stories as my legacy.

The Southern Gentleman

There is a breed of man indigenous to the South, and the breed is fading away even as we speak: the Southern gentleman. There are other species that seem to have overtaken this old breed, those who have a higher profile in the eye of society. The subsequent diminution in recognition is contributing to the demise of the species. The good ol' boy and even the redneck are better known—they get more attention in the media.

But I believe the Southern gentleman will endure. The characteristics that have stood him in good stead all these years are the characteristics that can survive. In fact, the true Southern gentleman seems to flourish in his semianonymity. Modesty is one of his most apparent characteristics.

The Southern gentleman may be the last bastion of masculine gentility to be found anywhere. He abhors the boastful demeanor that so many see as an expression of the male's grasp of his role in society, a role perceived as being just slightly above Cro-Magnon man.

He's as much at home driving a pickup truck as he is behind the wheel of a Cadillac. A Southern gentleman does not feel the need to make other people aware of his status in society. Instead, he chooses to let his daily interaction with his fellow man speak for him. He appreciates his neighbors for each one's attributes regardless of his race, religion, or social background.

There is much of the Renaissance man in the Southern gentleman. He has a broad interest in everything around him. He's appreciative and curious about the sciences and the nature of the world. He appreciates both the biological and the esthetic intricacies that comprise the universe. In many cases, he is a "son of the soil," a man tied to nature for his very existence. Subsequently, he is a religious man who has a strong faith in God and relies on that faith each time he plants his fields or his garden. He has a strong affection for God's handiwork—for the ocean, woods, streams, and their inhabitants.

He doesn't confine his athletic pursuits to the cumulative memory of sports statistics, but he appreciates the skill and effort that goes into achieving those statistics. He is aware of the need for the human body to reach and maintain a certain level of fitness, if only for the body to function at its maximum potential.

And when he clothes that body, he does so in a manner that shows his appreciation for tradition and for the dignity that comes from presenting himself well to other people.

A Southern gentleman appreciates the arts and is involved in some aspect of creativity that allows him to express the beauty of the language or languages we speak and the sights we see and the sounds we hear. Such an activity is not seen as unmasculine but an expression of the God-given talents we all possess.

A Southern gentleman has an appreciation for education that goes beyond his own personal achievements in that area. He believes that education is more than just the accumulation of facts, of information. Education is the ability to use all that we have accumulated and process it, to continue to ask questions until we reach our own conclusions through reason.

All of this belies the stereotype of the Southern gentleman as the master of the manor, content to sit on the veranda of his plantation house, sip bourbon, and talk about racehorses. Neither does it portray the scion of "the New South," one whose major role in life is the accumulation of wealth and power. He can be found most often in the small towns where the quality of life is defined more by the Sunday morning church service than the maneuverings of the boardroom.

These gentlemen are fading away. Each week I am reminded of their passing as I attend more funerals of such men. I am sorry to see them go. We'll probably never see their like again, and we will all be the lesser for it.

It will remain for those of us left behind—those of us born in a different time and in a different environment—to not merely revere the Southern gentleman as a memory of a bygone era but to continue to honor his legacy by emulating him.

I have spoken of the Southern gentleman many times over the years in my books and columns and speeches. Some things don't and shouldn't change.

The New Southern Belle

I do not usually write about women unless it is a profile about a specific woman. I try to avoid the topic of women in general, because women are so diverse in every way that any broad discussion often results in stereotypes that don't adequately describe the many individual characteristics of women. Therefore, it is with some trepidation that I embark on the subject, given my limited experience with women and even more limited understanding.

Having said all that, I can look back on my life and see that women have had a great influence on me. My mother was instrumental in forming my relationships with all people, particularly women. She often gave me good advice, which I didn't follow, but I learned something in the process—you learn from your mistakes.

I also absorbed information about the female species from my own planned and unplanned encounters. Though some people think it is impossible for men to develop a platonic relationship with a woman, I must disagree. I have and have had many women who were friends with no personal connection other than friendship. Sometimes those platonic friends were helpful in guiding me through the other kind of male-female relationships. But I digress.

Much of what I and many other people think women should be like, we got from books and the movies. Probably the most ingrained image of Southern womanhood came from the movie *Gone with the Wind*. It set out all the stereotypes we thought made up "women of the South."

There was the dutiful mother running the house, supervising the kindly, benevolent servants while the father served as "lord of the manor" and took care of the land and represented the family to the community. There was Melanie: sweet, kind, caring, always concerned with another's welfare even to the detriment of her own Mammy, the most caring of servants, tied to the family by a "benevolent slavery." Then there was the heroine, Scarlett O'Hara, whose major concern was the next party. She has had, by far, the greatest impact on the image of what a Southern belle was and is. Whether that image was ever actually accurate or not is still up for historians and sociologists to determine, but it certainly did exist in the minds of so many who saw the movie and translated the character on the screen to real life.

That image was one of self-interest—of parties and dances and picnics. It was an image that inextricably tied women's value to men, their social status, their wealth, their achievements. The fact that at the end of the movie, Scarlett is forced to rely on her own strength or resources is lost when Rhett Butler walks out the front door of Tara. Scarlett says, "I'll think about it tomorrow." Scarlett doesn't realize she is capable of prevailing over her own circumstances—or that she already has.

Today, there is a new Southern belle. She is her own person: confident, self-reliant, determined, assertive when necessary, and aware of the potential that she has within her to achieve her goals while accepting help but not relying on others. She generally is more educated, more informed, more aware of the circumstances that make up the world around her and the role she can play in that world.

All this is not to say that today's Southern belle has no interest in appearances. Every woman who has competed in the job market knows that how she looks makes a difference in how she is perceived. No matter how smart, educated, articulate, knowledgeable, competent, and otherwise qualified she might be, how she looks compared to other applicants is a major factor in determining who gets the job, whether the person doing the hiring is male or female. Right or wrong, that's the way it is.

Today's Southern belle is building on that tradition of unvoiced strength, of being the steel magnolia: silent, unobtrusive, but powerful. She is emerging as the leader, not just the power quietly pushing and supporting the leader but being the leader. My daughter, Mari, is a good example of this emerging image. She is thinking about writing a column that will extol the new Southern belle. There are of lot of potential subjects out there.

And what does this mean for us guys? It means we have to acknowledge the partnership.

MISS ESTHER AND THE HUSHPUPPIES

I have written about Miss Esther in other publications, particularly those that have to do with the South or, at least, our perception of it. Miss Esther Camaron was a Southern lady. She didn't fit any of the ordinary stereotypes that folks often associate with the term. I may have used a different name in writing about her sometimes, but Miss Esther was unique.

She was a very proud lady, but she had a kind of exuberant gentility that put those around her at ease. That could sometimes be seen in a nonstop narrative having to do with a recent community activity or the description of an encounter at the grocery store, a church service, woman's club gathering, or garden club meeting. That narrative often was accompanied by waving of hands and intimations of knowledge unknown to the rest of the world, as well as instructions not to repeat any part of the narrative. She loved to laugh and loved to make you laugh. That laughter sometimes belied a certain toughness that enabled her to rise above what could have been depressing circumstances.

Back in the early 1950s, my family owned a small oil distributorship in Hallsboro. Most of our business was providing fuel to farmers in the summer to fire their tobacco curers, and in the winter, we provided home heating oil, either kerosene or fuel oil. Miss Esther was one of our winter customers.

She lived in a big two-story house that, at one time, had been a real showplace. It was kept up nicely, but it had deteriorated some since its heyday back in the '20s. The Great Depression had adversely affected her family's finances, and her husband became a salesman for a local retail company. He had died right after World War II, and Miss Esther never held what she called a "public job." Her sole source of revenue was being a substitute English teacher and sometimes renting a room to "just the right kind" of tenant. She was also very frugal.

Even in her diminished financial situation, Miss Esther never lost her sense of "respectability"—the dignity of her perceived place in society—while still maintaining her ability to make everyone she met feel as if they were the most important person in her life at that specific time. In essence, she never stopped being a lady.

Each fall Miss Esther would call the oil plant and remind us it was time to fill her oil tank. I was usually the one to make the delivery, and almost always there would be some small maintenance of her heating equipment involved. One visit lingers in my memory.

She had an elegant dining room with a large fireplace at one end. She had covered the fireplace opening with a sheet of blue-painted plywood with a hole cut in it to accommodate a tin flue from a free-standing oil heater. On that delivery day, she wanted me to fit the flue through the wooden cover. I told her I'd have to put a flue collar on it to keep the wood from touching the hot flue. This did not fit into Miss Esther's esthetic ideals. She had painted the flue and the wood a dark blue, so she instructed me to paint the collar dark blue. Using the paint and brush she supplied, I painted the collar (which had been available but which she had chosen to ignore).

After I had painted the collar, I filled the fuel tank and installed the flue and new collar. On review, Miss Esther concluded that the blue on the collar was not exactly the shade of blue she wanted to match the blue plywood and, more importantly, the blue satin upholstery of the dining room chairs. I assured her that when the paint dried, it would match.

She said, "Well, William, it is teatime anyway, so why don't we have a bit of tea while we wait for the paint to dry?"

I was standing there with oil and soot all over me but knew better that to spurn Miss Esther's invitation. So I washed up at the sink on the back porch. When I returned to the dining room, my hostess had placed a silver tray and two glasses of iced tea on the table. She said, "Now William, I have some chocolate cookies or some of those little crackers if you would like, but I thought we might share a few of these hushpuppies I fixed yesterday."

So we did. Miss Esther and I sat there for quite a while talking about my plans for college. The English teacher and I talked about Emily Dickenson and Walt Whitman and Thoreau and Shakespeare. Then she talked about her personal reflection on "The War," an interchangeable term for "the War of Northern Aggression," and the two world wars. She talked about her grandfather who had fought for the Confederate army and had come back home to build up the farm. She talked of how the other wars had changed her life.

When we had finished our tea, hushpuppies, and conversation, she noted that the flue collar needed another coat of paint. I applied it, and she was satisfied.

I was not the only young person to come under the spell of Miss Esther.

For a while, she rented a room at her house to carefully chosen tenants. One was a young man named Johnny Hope, who worked at Boys and Girls Homes, which was right across the street from Miss Esther's house.

One summer my sister, Linda, worked at Boys Home and struck up an acquaintance with the young man who had rented the room in the old house. Naturally, since Linda was and is an attractive girl, Johnny asked Linda to go on a date. I don't know much about the date itself, but I do remember Linda telling me about her visit to Miss Esther's house and that Linda received very specific instructions on how a lady was supposed to act when visiting the residence of a young man. Miss Esther knew Linda well, so she gave that information freely without request or urging. She had rules like, "Ladies don't go into the parlor on the first meeting without a chaperone," and, of course, "Never go to his room."

My life has been well populated with ladies like Miss Esther, women who put a premium on dignity and decorum. Some might think such things are superficial, of little substance, reflect attitudes that are outdated. Those people might think those guidelines of interaction with others are not real virtues but a reflection of a time and place that no longer exist. Miss Esther was a product of that time and place, and that is not bad. Despite what modern doyennes may think, the ability to make others feel comfortable, to be hospitable in an often indifferent, cold world, never goes out of style. To make that happen, we need some guidelines. Rules of etiquette—good manners—are just guidelines to help us interact more easily with each other.

Miss Esther gave us all a road map to follow on the path to a more harmonious relationship with each other. I probably ought to write her a thank-you note, but it wouldn't be proper after all this time. Then again, Miss Esther taught us that an act of kindness or gratitude is always proper.

Miss Esther moved from the old house some time ago and has since died. The building eventually fell into ruin. Since then, I've eaten a lot of hushpuppies, but it's never been quite the same.

A Visit with Miss Lillie

I happened to see Jason at the drugstore the other day, and he told me that his mama, Miss Lillie, was visiting him. Jason and I have been friends since we were small children when Jason's family lived on my grandmother's farm in Chadbourn back in the 1950s. We used to go fishing together, and whatever we caught, Miss Lillie would cook for us. Best fish I ever ate.

When our families were "puttin' in" tobacco (harvesting, tying the leaves to sticks, and hanging them in the barn), Jason and I were in charge of picking up the fallen leaves of green tobacco that fell around the barn during the process. We were about five or six years old. Miss Lillie was the disciplinarian who sometimes gave us both a spanking for "fooling around" when we were supposed to be working.

Sometimes my grandmother would let me go with Jason and Miss Lillie to the African American Episcopal (AME) Zion church, which was just down the road from the farm. Miss Lillie sang in the choir, so she always put me and Jason on the front row so she could give us "the bad eye" if we misbehaved.

That all seemed like a long time ago as Jason and I stood there in the drugstore when he told me, "You oughta go see Mama. She'd love to see you. Just go on over to the house and surprise her." So I did.

Jason lives on a country road just a few miles from me. I knocked on the door of the little brick house but didn't get an answer, so I went around to see if Miss Lillie might be in the backyard. As I came around the corner of the house, I could hear her singing. I didn't recognize the song, but I could tell it was a gospel song from the lyrics: "Lord, keep me going down a lonesome road. I can't make it by myself ...." Miss Lillie was just singing away as she hung white bedsheets on a clothesline.

"Miss Lillie, Jason's got a washer and dryer in that house. What you doing with this clothesline?"

A startled Miss Lillie turned to see who had called her name. With a frown on her face she asked, "Who you?"

I should have known she wouldn't recognize me. It had been almost twenty years since she had left to live with her daughter in Baltimore and more years than that since she had seen me, but I was still kinda disappointed.

"It's William, Miss Lillie, from over at the farm in Chadbourn. Remember?"

"Oh my goodness, William. You sure changed. You 'bout scared me to death," she said as she rushed over and gave me a big hug. One thing I noticed right away: even after fifty years, Miss Lillie still smelled like talcum powder.

I may have changed a lot, but Miss Lillie hadn't changed much. She was still a tiny woman with short, cropped hair that had turned gray. She wore a simple print dress that hung loosely on her thin frame. She had on a pair of white socks stuffed into what looked like leather bedroom shoes.

"Lord, child, I didn't know what to think a White man come sneakin' up on me like that! You know I'm kinda timid anyway."

"Now, you know you're not timid, Miss Lillie. I remember you ran that tobacco barn crew like a drill sergeant. And you'd kill a snake with nothing but a garden hoe. And you sure didn't mind telling me and Jason what to do."

"Yeah, but y'all was good boys. You both turned out pretty good, so I musta done something right."

"We had good teachers like you, Miss Lillie."

"Come sit up here on the porch and tell me what you been doing."

Miss Lillie and I sat on the porch for a long time reminiscing about the days when our families worked together, when we all shared threats of too much rain or not enough, tobacco barns that caught on fire, boiling peanuts in a washpot in the backyard, fishing in a "creek" that was really just a wide ditch, funerals and weddings of both families.

"Those were good times weren't they, Miss Lillie?"

Miss Lillie didn't answer me right away. She sat in that rocking chair on her son's back porch and looked out across the cornfield at the sun brushing the top of the pine trees. Finally, she said, "They was good times if we want 'em to be, William. At the time, we all just did the best we could. Some of us fared better than others 'cause we didn't expect much so we wasn't disappointed. Sometimes we kinda picky 'bout what we remember. We just remember the good. Sometimes we even think the bad was good. All depends on how we want it to be, I reckon. That's the way I want it to be, William. I want it to be good."

Me too, Miss Lillie.

Defining the Good Ol' Boy

My publisher forwarded me an email the company had recently received regarding the book *Tuxedos and Pickup Trucks*. The reader, a lady who lives in Asheville, North Carolina, wrote, "I believe Mr. Thompson was being disingenuous in presenting himself as a 'good ol' boy' in his 'pseudo-memoir.' A person who is erudite enough to write as well as Mr. Thompson cannot possibly fit into that genre of male troglodytes who comport themselves in such a slovenly manner as to cast aspersions on the male species in general. However, even considering his misrepresentation, I enjoyed the book." The publisher said I may want to respond to this person.

Occasionally, I get letters or emails from readers about my writing. Usually, it is pretty straightforward: they like it or they don't. This woman probably gave me the most left-handed compliment I have ever received. I think I'm glad she liked it, but I had to look up some of the words she used just to make sure. As best I could tell, her main complaint about the book is that I did not portray "good ol' boys" in the negative light that she did. I haven't decided whether to contact her or not. However, I do believe she needed clarification.

I guess part of the problem this reader had was that she did not have a clear-cut definition of a good ol' boy. Like so many people, she confused them with rednecks. Having grown up in North Carolina, I have been and am acquainted with both groups and understand the slight nuances that separate the two. In defining the two groups, it is important to note that both groups are much like art, which is "in the eye of the beholder," and so is the perception of the two groups. It is important to note that the redneck and good ol' boy stereotypes overlap sometimes, which further complicates declaring an accurate definition. (I must confess I am probably in that overlapping group.)

Sometime ago, a psychologist friend of mine, Dr. David Cannon, gave me a scientific definition of a good ol' boy: "Good Ol' Boy (gudolboi) n. Male member of Genus Humorosus Hedonistus, Species Good Timus. Generally speaking, meets the following criteria: (1) fun-loving lifestyle, (2) humorous outlook, (3) unpretentious personal style. Found in all geographic locations and cuts across other sociocultural classifications."

The important part of that description is not so much in the delineation of the person himself as much as the statement that his species can be found anywhere. Over the years, many people—like my critic—have incorrectly assumed that they can identify a good ol' boy just by where he lives and how he looks. Although there are some unifying characteristics—blue button-down oxford cloth shirt, khaki pants, penny loafers or brown buckskin shoes, Red Man chewing tobacco in his back pocket and his pickup truck keys in another—those things alone do not a good ol' boy make. The best illustration I know of that belies the stereotype of appearance is when I saw a good ol' boy friend of mine dressed in a tuxedo as he arrived at a country club dance. Of course, it was a little incongruous to see him in that costume as he descended from the cab of his mud-covered four-by-four truck.

Although most folks think of good ol' boys as flocking together, to roost in bars and car repair shops, such is not the case. One of the best ways to determine a good ol' boy status is to look at his relationship to women.

First of all, good ol' boys genuinely like women—and not just sexually. Their first and eternal love is their mama, and woe be unto anyone who would disparage that woman in any way. Don't even try to shake the pedestal on which she stands!

Basically, good ol' boys are old-fashioned romantics who tend to fall in love very deeply. (I have never known a good ol' boy who had a little black book other than the Bible.) Having said that, it is important to note that his wife or sweetheart is not the only woman he likes. She may be the only woman he loves, but like the aforementioned man who appreciates art, he appreciates a lot of different kinds of paintings.

Another obvious characteristic of a good ol' boy that transcends other social designations is his speech. For instance, if the doctor, still clad in his white lab jacket, has completed his examination of the patient and says, "When your lab results come in, we'll give you a holler, Mrs. Fauntleroy," he is probably a good ol' boy.

Or, while being fitted for a new suit to wear to church, he tells the salesclerk, "I need something a little longer in the stride [crotch]."

Or, if he is the member of an industry-hunting group, he may report back to his committee that, "This new legislation is sure nuff efficacious in promoting capital formation of the basic industry sector."

Or, if he is a member of the legislature, he may say, "It is incumbent upon us as servants of the people to pass this public assistance bill. We cannot allow the poor families to root hog or die."

So I guess the lady from Asheville was wrong. I'm just an old red-necked good ol' boy. At least most of the time, I fit most of the above referenced criteria. I think I'll keep wearing my bow tie and driving my old pickup truck if I can get the door handle fixed.

A Tale of Three Fishermen

For several years, there has been a relatively unknown but prestigious fishing contest in this area of southeastern North Carolina. The coveted title is Perch Master. The title is a little nebulous in that it denotes the winner of a contest to see who can catch the most perch, including white perch, crappie, and shell cracker. It is also a contest involving total and singular weight. It is open to the public and held each spring around April or early May. The winner doesn't get a regular trophy; he earns bragging rights for a year. And though the contest may continue unofficially yearlong, the actual winner will stay the same until next year.

Over the years, there have been numerous entrants, but it seems that three Lake Waccamaw men were always the top contenders: Milton McLean, Louie Nye, and James Chavis. When McLean died, the group decided to pool whatever money was generated from the contest toward the installation of an osprey nest/box at Lake Waccamaw in memory of their friend. Because of the COVID-19 pandemic in 2021, the contest wasn't held, but the competition continues informally, at least between the two top contenders.

In a recent conversation with Nye and Chavis, it was easy to see they both shared a love for fishing, particularly the freshwater fishing available in the rivers and lakes of the area and specifically Lake Waccamaw. They also have an appreciation for their friend who was no longer there to add his pressure to the competition. Though his body had left this earth, his spirit was still alive on the lake. But beyond the competition, the two friends show a love for fishing.

"My granddaddy taught me how to fish," Chavis says. After all the serious instruction as to how to cast, where and how to find the fish, and the other general technical instructions, Chavis's grandfather gave him two specific instructions pertinent to the individual fisherman: "Always pray for God to help you, and then you gotta hold your mouth right." Both instructions are subject to individual interpretation. "But Milton taught me a lot, and Louis is always giving me tips. It's a real friendly competition," Chavis says.

On a particularly warm afternoon, Chavis and his son, Justin, are fishing at the dam where the Waccamaw River leaves the lake. The two take turns casting and reeling as the father continues to pass on his knowledge and love of fishing.

"We are Native Americans. We live out in the Saint James community," Chavis says. "Fishing is a part of who we are. It's important that I pass on this tradition to my son. I know the places where we can find the fish. One of the most enjoyable parts of fishing is eating the catch while it's still fresh. It just doesn't get any better than that!" he laughs.

Directly across the lake from Chavis, Louie Nye is casting for fish off the north shore and resting as the sun begins to set behind the cypress trees. The cool breeze coming off the lake creates easy waves lapping at the shoreline and brings a cool respite from the summer heat.

"Enjoying the lake like this is just as much a part of fishing as catching the fish," he says. "Being a native of this area is a blessing we don't take for granted. Not many folks can do this, be right here where it's peaceful and pretty and quiet. And if you happen to catch a fish under those circumstances, you are a blessed man."

But it would be a mistake to think that Nye is not an aggressive fisherman. "I look for 'em all over this lake, down at Big Creek, over at the Wildlife Park, the river mouth. I particularly look for the grass beds where the perch like to hide. Sometimes I'll mark the site so I can come back and try it later. I love catching fish. There is an excitement that can't be matched when you pull in a really nice size fish. You won the battle. Sometimes I just throw 'em back, let 'em get bigger, and try and catch 'em again. Then sometimes I'll keep and eat 'em right then or, at least, as soon as I get home."

In looking back at previous competition for the Perch Master title, Nye says: "It's always a lot of fun. We may have as many as twenty people come usually in April, which is the best time of the year to catch perch. We've never lacked for fish. Lake Waccamaw is great habitat for perch.

"I've been fishing this lake since I was a little boy. Billy Shipman taught me a lot about this lake and fishing. Some things have changed. There are more piers now and more people on the lake, and some runoff into the lake has caused some change. But it is still my favorite place to fish.

"Billy used to take me fishing, and we used a plain old cane pole, a cork, maybe some weights, a hook, and a worm on it. I still like to fish just about that same way. The fish haven't changed much, so I haven't changed the way I catch 'em."

Both fishermen share a sort of reverence for the lake. They see it not as just a place to catch fish, not just a site for a competition, but a part of their lives, a unique element that adds joy, relieves stress, and creates a sort of peace. They enjoy both the solitude and the camaraderie of other fishermen. Part of that camaraderie was their friendship with Milton McLean. He was a lot like them, maybe even a part of them. When they get that osprey box installed, they'll probably see it as a kind of physical connection that evokes the memory of fishing together, maybe an inspiration for more fish stories. Imagine that: fishermen telling fish stories.

(Listen to Bill recite this poem, track number 4 on Just Down the Road.*)*

In the Tracks of Daniel Boone

I saw him walking yesterday in the tracks of Daniel Boone
Up yonder where the Yadkin flows
In the glow of an autumn moon.

He walked with the bear, and none walked in fear,
And the leaves stirred,
And winter's breath drew near.

I saw him walking yesterday in the swamps,
In the wet, the dark, and the gloom.
He paid no mind to the gators and snakes
'Cause they gave him plenty of room.
'Cause the swamp was theirs where they'd shared a
Mutual womb.

I saw him walking yesterday, cookin' over an open fire.
To catch the biggest fish had been their hearts' desire.
And when his catch was placed o'er the flaming bier
He'd proved to his friends he wasn't a liar!

I saw him walking yesterday when he heard the rustle of quail.
They flushed from the brush; his dog was on their tail!
But he gazed long at the birds as they rose
And watched as they took sail.

Now, they say Ol' Daniel's gone to where there's elbow room,
That the woodsmen and the hunters spell the wildlife's doom.
But I believe Ol' Daniel's blood still flows in their hearts today,
'Cause I saw them walking side by side in the woods just yesterday.

Joe Dale's Boots

Growing up in a small rural community like Hallsboro, you meet a lot of "Joe Dales." They are the seldom seen and seldom heard. They live their lives quietly, routinely. Some might even say that their lives are boring. But caring about neighbors, providing for family, and serving God and country is not boring; it's inspirational. It's being what is known as "good people." I knew a lot of Joe Dales when I was growing up. They are more a part of my life than any famous people I met. Joe Dale is the everyman that is the heartbeat of life, the pulse of the community. My life would have been different without him.

Joe Dale's boots sat on the edge of the porch. Gray mud had oozed from the leather laces down over the whole boot and onto the wood of the weathered porch. It was a seamless sheet of muck, a combination of dirt and manure and swamp water. The cold wind that swept across the field in front of the house had dried the whole mess, smoothing it out until it looked like it had been sculpted then welded to the wood. If you'd had a mind to, you could have just picked up the whole thing and set it on top of Joe Dale's tombstone. It would have been like an unwritten epitaph.

They were the government-issue boots Joe Dale had worn when he came home from Korea.

He had worn those boots when he followed our old mule, plowing up the new ground down next to the swamp.

He had worn them when he, Myles Cowan, and Daddy walked across the stubble of the soybean field, watching Ol' Dan with his nose to the ground, looking for quail.

He had worn them when he stood two rows over from the auctioneer as his tobacco crop was auctioned off for the last time at the old warehouse in town.

He had worn them down through the swamp, bumping them against the cypress knees when he had to chase the old sow and pigs back up to the broken pen at Uncle Fred's place.

He had worn them when he had to pick up his son Joseph at school when the boy was suspended for smoking cigarettes outside of the school's designated smoking area. Joe Dale had thought that was kind of ironic, seeing as how tobacco had helped pay for the school.

He had worn them when he sorted through what was left of his house and barns after Hurricane Hazel came through and after, when he and his neighbors rebuilt everything.

He had worn them down to Simmons Mill Pond, where he hardly ever caught any fish but did a lot of quiet relaxing.

He was wearing them that day when his heart gave out on him as he was coming back from cutting up an old tree for winter firewood over at Miss Ella's house.

Those old boots told a lot about Joe Dale, their frayed laces having woven through the muddy water and dust of his life, tying the insignificant and meaningful together.

Two Grandfathers at Christmas

The old man had been waiting at the bus station in Lumberton since early that morning. It was almost noon when I saw him there. He wore faded overalls and a denim overall jacket. His hat was the familiar baseball cap with a John Deere logo on the front; his shoes, a pair of high-top sneakers.

I watched him for a while, wondering who he was waiting for. As I went to pick up my package, he walked over to the trash can and threw in a soft drink can and several Slim Jim wrappers.

Finally, my curiosity got the best of me, and with an apology for my brashness, I asked him what would make him wait so long on a cold December day. "My granddaughter," he said without looking at me. "She's coming to stay with me at Christmas."

Now in this part of the country, "stay with me" could mean a short visit or a permanent residency. He didn't say "for Christmas," just "at Christmas."

"Sure she wasn't on that earlier bus?" I asked.

"No," he said. "It ain't due yet. But I wanted to be sure and be here when she got off."

The old man kept his eyes focused down the street from which the bus would arrive. He backed up to the wall of the station and placed one foot against the building, then pulled out a bag of pork skins from his pocket and began to eat them.

I noticed that his hands were puffy and wrinkled, and in the creases were traces of oil or grease. His fingernails had been cut short, but you could still see evidence of dirt under them. As he munched on the pork skins, I noticed he had just a few teeth left.

"Worked all my life for my children," he said without my inquiry. "That's all we ever have you know, your young'uns. Clarise, my wife, passed away four years ago this June. My oldest boy got killed in Afghanistan, and my other'n is in service somewhere over that way now. This granddaughter comin' is the daughter of the one what got killed."

That's all he said. I thought it was nice of his granddaughter to spend her Christmas vacation with her grandfather. I left the old man by wishing him a Merry Christmas, and I went back to my car.

***

I have often written about my grandfather, Dave Council, in my books and columns over the last several years. He was a unique man in many ways. When he was still very young, his mother secured the assistance of a storekeeper family in Hallsboro to help raise her only son. She had four other older children at home and felt she couldn't give him the kind of "raisin'" she wanted to give him. Mrs. Pierce, his surrogate mother, had been a schoolteacher at a time when schoolteachers could not be married. (I don't know what the logic was.) My grandfather became her only student. So she had plenty of time to give my grandfather the benefit of her teaching ability and knowledge.

After watching some of the recent political squabbles on television and contemplating the diminution of what I perceive to be the Christmas spirit, I was reminded of a quote I heard him use many times as he and my father and uncles discussed political affairs on the porch at his house on Sunday afternoons. It came from a fellow named James Truslow Adams, a businessman turned historian around the turn of the twentieth century. (I had to look that up.) I don't know if Mrs. Pierce was aware of Mr. Adams, but I do know my grandfather quoted him. It was an applicable statement a hundred years ago and still applies today. He said, "There is so much good in the worst of us, and so much bad in the best of us, that it ill behooves any of us to find fault with the rest of us." That thought holds its own Christmas spirit.

Some of my fondest memories of my grandfather are tied to Christmas, which, in a small town, attaches itself inextricably to the essence of who we become. It is something we celebrate forever, long after the designated celebration has ceased. Some Santas have a unique persona. My Santa still looks a lot like my Grandfather Council.

I remember one year it didn't look much like Christmas. The smoke from the lumber mills had mixed with the fog, and intermittent light rain cast a gray cover over the little town of Hallsboro. Despite the gloomy weather, the Christmas spirit prevailed.

It was 1956, and all the mills were doing a booming business. The little stores, including my family's general store, were decorated with colored lights around the doors and small show windows. Somebody had spelled out "Merry Christmas" in white glitter paint on one of the windows of the little soda shop.

But inside our store was an even more festive atmosphere. We had cut a pine tree from the woods right behind the store and placed it on one side of the store next to the appliances. My sister, mother, and Aunt Lucille let me help decorate it. It wasn't like the classic Christmas fir tree. It was a pine with significant gaps between the limbs, and it leaned a little no matter how you turned it. But it was pretty: big colored lights that blinked, a long string of stale popcorn wrapped around from the bottom to the top with tinsel icicles randomly placed all over, solid glass balls of red and green hanging tenuously from the spindly pine needles, and a gold star on the top. Mama and Aunt Lucille questioned the aesthetic appeal, but sister Linda and I thought it looked great.

We sold record players in the store, not stereos or sound systems but record players that played 33 ⅓ long-playing records, as well as the small 45 rpm singles.

That day we had put on a recording of Christmas music and turned up the sound loud enough to be heard all over the store.

Toys were displayed on shelves and tables along the side of the store. Cap guns and air rifles were placed right beside basketballs and footballs and dolls and checkerboards and Monopoly games. And shiny bikes with whitewall tires!

But it was the grocery side of the store that really told you it was the Christmas season. The produce section was filled with oranges and apples and grapes and bananas and dried dates … and collards and sweet potatoes and Irish potatoes and cabbages and celery. And right at the end of the produce counter was a special section of Christmas candy: hard candy with peppermint and hot cinnamon flavors and sticks of licorice and orange slices and my daddy's favorite chocolate-covered cherries. All those smells from the fruits and candy mingled with the music and the Christmas tree lights and the toy display to create a magical feel that couldn't be duplicated, even in a grand store like Macy's in New York.

It was into this wonderful, captivating atmosphere that Clarence Henderson came. My family knew him. My Grandfather Council had run the company store for one of the lumber companies before opening his own store. He had seen Clarence many times on the mill site where he worked as an oiler—the man who kept the saws and conveyor belts and everything else that turned turning.

It was almost closing time when he came in. I could smell the oil on him when he came in the door. It was such a heavy smell. I could almost see it rise around him through the flakes of sawdust that covered his bibbed overalls and flannel shirt. A tiny stream of water ran down a crease in his wide-brimmed hat that had long ago lost its shape, and his high-topped brogan shoes daubed mud on the floor with every step he took.

"Evening, Clarence. What can I do for you?" my grandfather asked.

"Well, I don't rightly know, Cap'n," he responded. Cap'n was a title that denoted no rank but was a common name for any man who had supervised laborers at the mill. "I gotta git some Christmas for my brother Chance's family. You know he got busted up pretty bad when that log chain broke the other day down in the swamp. That thing flew back and wrapped 'round his legs, you know. Broke both of 'em. He's stove up bad. Ain't worked in a couple o' weeks, so he ain't got nothing for them kids for Christmas."

My grandfather did know the circumstances of the Henderson family and was a sympathetic and generous man, so his immediate response was, "Tell you what I'll do, Clarence. You go ahead and pick out what you think'll make a good Christmas, and we'll just make it a gift to you to help out."

Clarence didn't respond immediately. He just stood there and looked down at the floor as the Christmas music from the record player provided accompaniment for his thoughts.

Finally, he said, "Cain't do that, Cap'n. You see, if you give the stuff to me, it'll be your present, not mine. Them children is family. I got to do this myself."

Then he reached in the pocket of his old overalls and pulled out a handfull of change. "This is what I got. You know I cain't cipher. You count it out and tell me what I can get for it," he instructed.

My grandfather took the change, counted it, and said, "There's a dollar and twenty-one cents here. That'll buy a pretty good Christmas."

So Clarence began to gather items in his arms. There was no shopping cart, no basket, just his big arms. He gathered some oranges and apples and then stopped at the candy counter as he looked at what he had gathered and then at my grandfather. "'Nough left for some candy?" he asked.

"Oh yes. You got a lot left," was the response.

So Clarence picked out a few pieces of the hard candy and a couple of orange slices and brought his armload to the cash register and placed it on the counter. As he looked over on the side of the store at the toy display, he asked, "You reckon there's enough left to get the two little ones a toy apiece?"

"Oh, I think so," was the almost whispered response.

Clarence picked out a yo-yo for the boy and a Raggedy Ann doll for the girl and brought them to the counter. "What does all that come to, Cap'n?"

My grandfather pushed some buttons on an adding machine and said, "That comes to exactly a dollar and twenty cents." Then he reached in his pocket and took out a penny. "And here's your change."

All of the items were placed in a paper bag. As he lifted the bag and stepped toward the door, he said, "Thank you, Cap'n. Y'all have a nice Christmas now."

I watched Clarence get in his car and drive away from the store. The sputter of the engine and the rattle of the old car seemed to fit in with the fog and the rain. But then again, it could have been sleigh bells.

***

As I was preparing to leave the bus station that night in Lumberton, the bus pulled in. I waited to see what the meeting of the grandfather and granddaughter would be like. The old man didn't move from the building, but in a few minutes, the bus driver came over and said something to him, and the two of them went on the bus. In just a minute, the old man emerged, and with him was a little girl about ten years old. She had on a pandemic mask, so I couldn't see her features, but she ran over to the old man and took his hand.

In deference to COVID, there were no hugs and kisses, but the little hand was clasped tightly in the rough and wrinkled hand of the old man. As they walked away from the bus station, I thought at least a part of his son was home for Christmas.

You Can Move Away, But You Can Never Leave Home

Dalton Bernard Dockery's roots go deep in Columbus County soil. His maternal ancestors, the Stanlys, lived in the Nakina area more than two hundred years ago and, after World War II, became one of the earliest African American families to own their own land. That distinction was not only a sign of their independence but also inspired them to survive on the land, as well as improve and preserve their land so future generations would be a part of it.

Doris, Dalton's mother, remembers her father's divinely inspired statement, "Blessed is he who owns his own land." Dalton recalls that his grandfather, Malachi Stanley, enlisted in the army in 1942 during World War II and was discharged in 1945 with the rank of private. During that time, the Army was segregated, and he served as a cook. On returning home from service in the US Army, he, along with two of his siblings, purchased 350 acres of wooded land in the Nakina area. Out of the 350 acres, he ended up with about 100 acres to farm.

Dalton noted that: "In the late 1940s, many African American farmers were sharecroppers or tenants of White farmers. So for them to purchase so much land at one time was an accomplishment in and of itself. During that time, this was considered a nice size farm for an African American farmer to actually own and not rent."

But farming was not to be the only legacy of Dalton's family. Education was a primary element. Dalton's grandmother, Edna, married Malachi

Dalton and, shortly after, attended and graduated from the nearest Black college, Fayetteville State University. She later earned her master's degree in Elementary Education from North Carolina Agricultural and Technical State University (NC A&T). Because there were few jobs for Black teachers in the county, she had to go to Georgia to get a job but later returned to teach as the first African American teacher at Old Dock Elementary School.

In those early days, land ownership for everyone carried not only distinction and unique status but also carried with it a challenge to provide from the land everything the family needed. The house and barns, as well as fuel for cooking and warming the house, came from the trees on the farm. The food came from the large gardens and a wide range of livestock, plus what could be harvested from the wildlife in the woods and the fish in the rivers and streams. Farming was a very self-sufficient lifestyle for everyone, Black and White. There was no electricity and little machinery. Mules were the primary assistants in tilling the soil.

According to Doris: "We all worked together on each other's farms. There was not much social life to integrate; there was just work, church, and school. We went to different churches and different schools."

However, she was in the first group to integrate Nakina High School. "We were aware of the differences, but it was not overwhelming," she notes.

Doris also attended Fayetteville State, where she met her husband, Leon Dockery, obtained a degree in special education, and went on to be a teacher like her mother before her. "Back then in our families and many others, it was just understood that the girls would go to college and the boys would go to work when we got out of high school," Doris says.

Of course, that tradition changed, and as for Bernard—the name Dalton's family calls him—it was already decided that he would go on to college after he graduated from Nakina High School. Leon also graduated from Fayetteville State University with a bachelor's degree in math education, and he was the first Black male teacher at Nakina and still maintains relationships with many of his former students.

Dalton is the oldest of four children born to Doris and Leon Dockery. He has two sisters, Andre and Courtney, and a brother, Jason, who died young. Andre and Courtney completed college and are pursuing successful careers in Charlotte. Courtney is a former Miss Columbus County.

"Bernard set the bar high," was the statement from his siblings. In listening to the conversation among the Dockerys, a visitor gets the feeling that they are all mutually supportive of each other, sharing a certain pride in each other's achievements. Part of that mutual feeling is an appreciation for home, not just for each other but for the people, past and present, who influenced their lives.

"This is home, and that is really important to me," Dalton assures. "I had opportunities to go elsewhere, but I chose to stay here," he says. That is not to say that those roots didn't produce a quality life. Dalton was director of the Columbus County Cooperative Extension Service, then became Southeast district extension director. He has a bachelor's degree in education from NC State University and a master's degree in agricultural and extension education from NC State as well. He also received his PhD in leadership studies from NC A&T. He recently retired as president of the NC Agricultural Extension Service.

"Even at a time when the civil rights movement was at its height, my grandfather was a 4-H [youth group] volunteer and in charge of a 4-H club. His love of agriculture and his fellow man was a tremendous reflection of our core family values that remain today."

Dalton will be the first to tell you that his proudest achievement is his family. He just celebrated the twenty-fifth anniversary of his marriage to his wife, Shelia, who is the director of financial aid at Southeastern Community College. His daughter, Whitley, is very academically and musically talented and has participated in many local performances. And his son, Bryson, has become somewhat of a local celebrity since taking a particular interest in the US Constitution and producing a show on Facebook to demonstrate his interest and get other people involved. As evidence of his success in this endeavor, he recently participated in a forum with the secretary of the NC Department of Education. Not only is his family proud of him, but so is everybody else in Columbus County!

It is especially important to note that Dalton has taken the lead in providing leadership in a time when race relations are a major part of the lives of all Americans. As he has always done, he has focused on finding ways to create unity here at home. He wants to bring people together, to discuss our differences, and to emphasize those things that bind us. He organized a peaceful prayer demonstration in Whiteville that was successful, and he is still looking for ways to bring us all together.

In looking back over his lifetime, Dalton made some extraordinary observations. He said, "Our story, and the story of most African American farmers that come from the corridors of slavery, was a major milestone in the civil rights movement. Many of the children who once walked the dusty roads of our Nakina community have gone on to achieve great things. My grandparents realized that education is the future for generations. I never would have dreamed that fifty years after my grandmother finished NC A&T State University with a master's degree that I would attend the same college and complete a PhD degree in leadership.

"The generations of African American children who were raised on the farms in Nakina have gone on to be lawyers, doctors, educators, etc. Nakina, no matter its shortcomings, was the best place to grow up. It is safe to say that 95 percent of all the children, Black and White, who grew up in Nakina have been successful in life. That makes my hometown special. It is still hard for me to believe that I am only five or six generations from my enslaved forefathers."

That's how it is when roots run deep in your community.

Everybody Has an "Old Place"

When I was growing up, I would hear my mother's family talk about "The Old Place." For a long time, I figured that place was just an old house that sat in a field about four hundred yards behind my grandparents' house. I assumed it was called that because it was old. I was a teenager before I learned that The Old Place was more than just a building; it was where my great-grandmother and great-grandfather lived and where my mother and three of her siblings were born.

By the time I understood the significance of the place, it had been relegated to use as a pack house for storing tobacco until it could be prepared for sale. I remember playing under the trees in what remained of a yard as my mother and aunt and some other ladies carefully graded and tied the dried tobacco leaves prior to the golden leaf being taken to the auction warehouse in Whiteville. I remember rambling through the old house, unmindful of the weak floorboards and the broken pieces of glass.

But later I became curious about the old house and began to ask endless questions about it. I learned that the small building that sat behind the house had once been connected by a covered porch to the rest of the house. That building was the kitchen, and it was set away from the rest of the house to prevent fire from spreading from the more flammable kitchen.

I learned that the pile of wood with a keyboard on the living room floor was the remains of an old pump organ that my great-grandmother used to play. When I asked about that old instrument, I learned that my Great-grandfather Flynn used to play the fiddle for square dances around Hallsboro just as my Grandfather Thompson had played over toward Chadbourn. Being a good Baptist, I wondered how the family had justified playing for dances since, at that time, such activity was considered sinful by that denomination. My Grandmother Council said they could always ask forgiveness.

My Great-grandmother Flynn died when my Grandmother Zadie was born. So that left her an only child to be raised by a single father. Grandpa Flynn never remarried. I heard many stories from my grandmother about how she took care of the house and learned to cook at an early age. She said there were few female family members close by, but her mother's aunts helped out until she took over. (My Great-grandmother Flynn was a Thompson. Long story.)

When Grandmother was born, Grandpa Flynn built another bedroom onto the house. Then when Grandmother married my Grandfather Council, the newlyweds moved into the newest bedroom. Then along came my Uncle Wilbur, and he had to share Grandpa's room. Then my Aunt Lucille was born, and they divided Grandpa's room. Uncle Charles shared that room with Uncle Wilbur and Grandpa until my mother came along and they decided they needed another house. So they bought the old teacherage at Red Bug School and left The Old Place.

My family, like most farm families, adapted reluctantly. Although Grandpa Flynn had a room in the new house, sometimes he would sleep over at The Old Place. He said he needed some peace and quiet away from a house with four rambunctious children less than six years of age. By the time Uncle Carl was born, Grandpa had died, and the boys all shared a room, and the girls shared a room.

Mama was the youngest child and the first to get married. I became the oldest grandchild and never knew Grandpa Flynn. But I've been told I'm a lot like him. I wish I had known him. Maybe I'd understand myself better.

The Old Place burned several years ago, and the land was sold. But I remember going over there to pick up pecans from the big trees. My mother loved reading and writing poetry, and she loved The Old Place. So several years ago, I wrote a poem about the place for her birthday. I don't think she'd mind if I shared it.

(Listen to Bill recite this essay and poem, track number 8 on Just Down the Road.*)*

The Old Place

There's a place not far from here where people seldom go;
it's a place that's never seen the light of the neon glow.
'Bout the only way you can get there now
is to get folks who lived there to show you how.

In a time not long ago there was a small farm
where a family lived safely hidden from harm.
With a mule and a cow, some pigs and a dog or two
plus three sons and two daughters before they were through.

The wife kept house plus a whole lot more
while the father took care of a country store.
They all stayed busy, never got bored,
and only asked for help from The Lord.

As time went on, each left that place,
packed their bags and turned their face
toward lives full of hope and joy and things.
They shared a bond that only family brings.

Now "The Old Place" is gone, fire didn't leave much,
just memories of good times and love and such.
But some thoughts never leave, gives your heart a tug,
when we think how things were back in Red Bug.

A Soldier's War Is Personal

There is no glory in war. There is honor and duty and sacrifice, but there is no glory in the foxholes and trenches, the lonely skies, the roiling seas, the burning sands, or stifling jungles. For some, like me, there is the assurance that God is with them, but there is no romantic poetry that can glorify the death of the friend next to you who gets his head blown off, his blood and brains covering you.

I believe that was how Bryant Powell felt as he fought in the jungles of Vietnam and how many soldiers in wars throughout history felt as well. Bryant was the first Boys Home of North Carolina boy to die in a war. There have been many since, and each one left behind people they loved and people who loved them—and lots of memories.

Bryant Powell and Anne Wyche were sweethearts in high school here in Hallsboro. He was a tremendous athlete who could have gone on to play in college, but he chose the military. When he left to go to California then to Vietnam, he went by Salem College, where Anne was a student, to tell her goodbye. She would never see him again. But they would write letters to each other. Anne kept her letters all these years until she agreed to share them with me as part of the history of Boys and Girls Homes that I am writing. Here are some of the excerpts from Bryant's letters.

USS Iwo Jima, *July 18, 1966: Well, I am in Hawaii. It is beautiful here. We are getting ready to pull out. We are coming back here someday.*

USS Iwo Jima, *July 25, 1966: I am sitting on a box in my compartment that has 4 shotguns and about 30.45 caliber pistols and a rack of 14 rifles. Mine is hanging on my rack. I go to bed at night and look over at my rifle. I know that the games and the kid stuff is over. This is the real thing. I get scared and all screwed up inside when I say my prayers and think about life at home and the lake ....*

USS Iwo Jima, *July 29, 1966: I want to get back to the States alive and in one piece because I have a lot to live for and look forward to. I can't wait to get to the lake and get all the old gang and have a good time again down at Susan's lake beach or going down to your lot and playing with the ducks and going swimming and laying in the sun. When I get home, I'm going to throw the most unusual party you have ever seen at Lake Waccamaw!*

August 22, 1966: It is 42 miles southeast of Saigon ... I am scared to death, the most scared I have ever been in my life but I have got the will to live. There is a lot of activity in our squad bay tonight. Usually, it is quiet but the tension is so high, it seems like people just can't wait to go hunting for the gooks. Pray for me.

Bryant went out into the jungles of Vietnam because that was his duty. He was a soldier, and that's what soldiers do. As I watch the exodus of our troops from Afghanistan, I am reminded that we went into that faraway country to fight initially because we had been attacked by terrorists who were based in that country. We succeeded in avenging the attack on America, and we stayed because we thought we could help that country become like us, a democratic society. Not everybody agreed with the reason, but every soldier who went there did so because he was a soldier, an American soldier, who does his duty—just like Bryant did.

On October 6, 1966, Bryant sent Anne a letter describing being shot at by Vietcong as he was trying to load wounded soldiers into a helicopter.

Bryant Russell Powell, 3rd Marine Division, 1st Battalion, 26 Marine, D Company from Lake Waccamaw, North Carolina, was killed by a sniper on October 11, 1966. He was twenty-one years old.

There are twenty-seven letters in all. Each one asks for prayer. We usually offer prayers for soldiers on Memorial Day and Veterans Day. Let us pray for all soldiers who do their duty every day because they are soldiers.

Bryant and Anne's story took place in hundreds of towns and cities across America. But the small-town heart seems more susceptible to loss—at least to small-town people.

The Pink Rocking Chair

My friend J.B. had wanted me to come by to see him, so I did. It wasn't easy getting to his house. I had to leave the paved road and follow the sandy Onslow County road for about a mile through some cutover woodland and across a wooden bridge that his father made back in the 1920s.

J.B. told me, "Papa built that bridge when he bought his first car. Didn't need a bridge for a mule and wagon to cross that swampy spot. Built it out of solid oak boards he cut right here on the farm."

Those same boards put there at the end of World War II were still there, give or take a board or two, for me to cross that day.

When I crossed the bridge, I could see J.B. out in the front yard of his little house. It was the house he had been born in almost ninety years ago. When he was fifteen years old, he had left it and his family there near Hubert to follow the horse show circuit as a groom for a wealthy man from Jacksonville, NC. During that time, he had done well for himself financially, saving his money and making good investments. He had come back home upon retirement.

I asked him once why, with all his money, he hadn't retired to Florida or some other place other than Hubert. "I saw all I wanted to see of Florida and most everywhere else. I hadn't seen enough of home," he answered.

As I got out of the car and started walking toward the house, I could see that J.B. was painting a rocking chair. He had placed it on two cement blocks right out in the yard and was applying the pink paint with a small paintbrush.

I thought it was curious that this man would want a pink rocking chair for that particular house. The sides of the house had turned gray from weather and age. The porch that went across the front of the house was about three feet off the ground, and you could see under it where a couple of dogs were resting. Only one of the windows, the one for the bedroom, had any curtains.

J.B. looked a lot like the house. What hair he had was gray, and he wore a pair of gray corduroy slacks, a faded blue shirt with the sleeves rolled up, and an old pair of lace-up riding boots.

We greeted each other, shook hands, and he invited me to come and sit on the porch with him. I wanted to ask him right then why he was painting that rocking chair pink but was afraid it might embarrass him, and I figured if he wanted me to know, he'd tell me later.

He poured himself a glass of water from a jar filled with ice water and asked me if I wanted some. I told him I did. J.B. had told me long ago that he believed in drinking a lot of water. No soft drinks and definitely no alcohol. He said that was one reason he was still healthy at his age.

We talked for a good while about the business he had called to talk about. Then he reminisced for a while, as always when we were together, about the old days when he was traveling as a groom with the wealthy man's horses.

I was getting ready to leave, and as we walked toward the car, he asked, "Aren't you going to ask me about the pink rocking chair?"

"Well, I am curious," I said. "But I figured you'd tell me if you wanted me to know."

"I knew you wouldn't ask. You're too polite sometimes. You are one of the few people who ever comes to see me, so I'll tell you. Hardly anybody ever comes up here to talk to me, like I didn't really come back home, like I'm a stranger or something. I figure that when I die, folks will come up here and see that pink rocking chair. They'll wonder why an old man like me would have a piece of furniture that color. They will speculate and propose all kinds of reasons, none of which will be true. I painted it so they will have something to talk about and remember when I'm gone, even if they wouldn't talk to me when I was living."

J.B. died a few months after my visit. I went to his funeral, and sure enough, the main topic of conversation at the graveside service was the pink rocking chair. I never told anybody his reason for painting the chair.

Evelyn Booker, Pioneer Broadcaster

Like most people of achievement, Evelyn Smith Booker got off to a rough start. She was born at home on a farm in Nakina. For the first couple of days she just slept, didn't eat or do any of the things most babies do. But like so many things in her life, she credits divine intervention with waking her up to start a life that would take her from the fields of Nakina to the head of a major television operation.

When she retired in March 2011, she had spent thirty years with Capitol Broadcasting in Raleigh. She had risen through the ranks from assistant copywriter at WRAL TV to a management position at a Fortune 500 company, the top of the corporate ladder, interacting with executives nationally and around the world.

But she never forgot her roots or what she had learned while climbing the ladder of success. Early on, her parents and Sunday school teachers gave her some simple guidelines such as, *No matter what, always do your best. Believe in yourself. Respect yourself and others. Speak with confidence and conviction. Master the English language.*

She took those lessons with her as she faced life's challenges. Among her first challenges was being one of the first African American students to integrate Nakina High School. She not only made the transition but also graduated at the top of her class.

After a brief start at NC Central University, she came home to take care of her ailing mother. After her mother's recovery, she returned to the university, met her future husband, Lee Booker, got a bachelor of arts degree in English and a minor in education, and learned some more about life, including, *Put your trust in the Lord. Don't wear your feelings on your sleeve. Study. Mind your own business. Be cautious with whom you associate.*

When Booker went to work for Capitol Broadcasting, she practiced all the lessons she had learned. Most of it boiled down to working hard and always looking at a situation from two personal viewpoints: hers and her clients'. The goal was to bring those viewpoints close together. Part of her career was spent mentoring others, so it was natural that at her retirement, there were so many who spoke her praises.

One of those speakers, Leon Duncan, senior vice president of hospitality and entertainment for the Washington Redskins, said, "The day I went to work for Evelyn Booker marks one of, if not the most, pivotal moment in my life. She was my mentor, my relationship counselor, my spiritual adviser, and my moral compass." Similar sentiments have been expressed by many who went on to become top executives in high-powered companies.

In January 2021, Kevin Hungate of NBC Universal, and one of Booker's first hires at WRAL TV in Raleigh, arranged for her to be interviewed by the nonprofit advocacy group Black and Brilliant in a partnership event with BOLD at NBC Universal to create a conversation about mentoring and paying it forward. And she has written a book, *A Winner in Spite of,* in which Kevin Hungate said, "She shares a bit of her personal story and worklife [and] a little of her philosophy, drops in a dollop of motivation, dispenses practical wisdom, and, above all, celebrates her faith and puts God at the center of absolutely everything."

And it all started on a little farm in Nakina.

Freddie Stell: A Star in a Community of Characters

All the world's a stage,
And all the men and women merely players;
They have their exits and their entrances;
And [each person] in his time plays many parts.

That's what Shakespeare said. Casting Fredrika Stell in the one proper role in her life in theater and the Columbus County community would be a real challenge even to Shakespeare. She has such a varied background and so many talents that narrowing them all down to one character would be almost impossible—even for Freddie, who has chosen the casts for so many stage productions.

She easily could have been Maria from *The Sound of Music*; she wrote plays and involved her younger neighbors in Clarkton when she was just a little girl.

She could have been Ado Annie in *Oklahoma*, since she always saw the good and the unique potential of all who wanted to come under the thespian spell. "I love to hear audience laughter," she once said.

Or she might have been Anna in *The King and I*, determined to teach understanding and respect and love.

She did have a role in a production of *Steel Magnolias* as M'Lynn, the mother who is so strong and stubborn and always knows best.

She was involved in each of those plays. All of those characteristics make up the person of Fredrika Turner Stell. Perhaps the title "grande dame" would fit her too. Such a title is given to a woman who dominates or has great influence in a particular area like theater, a kind of matriarch. Freddie certainly was all that. I asked her once how long she had been involved in Columbus County theater. She responded, "Oh, I don't know. A long time."

She was instrumental in organizing the Columbus County Theater Association, which assembled dramatic, comedic, and musical productions. When asked if she had a favorite genre, she said, "No, I like them all. But if I had to choose, I'd pick those that made the audience laugh. It just makes me feel good to hear the laughter and know that I made them feel good, if only for a little while."

Because of Freddie's involvement in theater in Columbus County, she has given so many people a chance to expand their confidence in themselves and to look at the performing arts as more than something to watch. "You know, there are a lot of 'closet' actors, people who don't think they can perform on stage, but given the chance and the encouragement, they do a great job. Understanding the role, the character they are portraying, expands their understanding of other people offstage."

Freddie's approach to directing has made it possible for many people to come out of their shell. "When a person gets on stage, they become somebody else for a little while. They can do and say things that they wouldn't do or say otherwise. That has always given me a great deal of satisfaction when I see that happen. That means they are actors in the real sense of the word," she said.

Sometimes, Freddie's productions brought whole families onto the stage. "Rehearsals that involved children and their parents were always interesting," she said. "Sometimes I would have to assert my directorship to keep everybody focused, but it was always worth it. We would see everything going wrong, worry about sets and sound and inevitable conflicts of schedule, but it always came together. There sometimes were different levels of success, but I believe that every production we ever did was a hit, as far as I'm concerned.

"People are always asking me when I'm going to do another play, and I tell them I'll be glad to help anybody who wants to put one on, *help* being the key word. We are so fortunate to have such an active high school performing arts program. It would be nice if we could revive play productions for everybody. I've told everybody that asked me about doing plays again that I'll be glad to help."

Sadly, Freddie passed away in 2021.

In retrospect, Fredricka Stell may not have been a grande dame. That title connotes a sense of haughtiness, maybe even a little bit of elitism. That is surely not Freddie Stell. She was more like a grand dame than a *grande dame*. She was unique. And after all, as they said in *South Pacific*, "There is Nothin' Like a Dame."

GARLAND McCULLEN

Garland McCullen is a son of the soil, a man who appreciates the land and the people who tend it. He grew up with three brothers on a farm in Sampson County. Like all farm families, they worked together to raise the crops and livestock. He learned a strong work ethic early on and continued to follow it for the rest of his life.

While still in high school, he rented an acre of tobacco from a neighbor, tended it all season, and bought his first car with the money made from the sale of the tobacco.

He originally wanted to be a veterinarian, but during the course of study at Campbell College, where he received his associate degree, he decided to follow a different route. So he attended NC State University and earned a bachelor of science degree in soil science and later his master's degree in education.

He was working with the Moore County agriculture extension office when he met Charlie Raper, who was the extension agent in Columbus County at that time. Mr. Raper talked to him about coming to work in Columbus County.

"Lake Waccamaw impressed me so much, I decided to take Mr. Raper's offer," McCullen remembers. It was 1965 when young McCullen became the director of the 4-H program in the county. He would hold that position for ten years. In that time, the 4-H program and the young people in it were recognized for their accomplishments.

"But it wasn't until I retired that I received the greatest honor of my life," McCullen says. In 2009, long after his retirement, McCullen was inducted as a charter member of the NC 4-H Hall of Fame.

McCullen worked as the 4-H agent for ten years under Mr. Raper, and in 1975, upon Mr. Raper's retirement, McCullen became the extension agent for Columbus County. He held that position for twenty years until his retirement in 1995.

"I always considered the staff as co-workers," he says. "Each of us had certain assigned responsibilities, but whenever the need arose, we all worked together to accomplish any task."

During that time, he saw many changes in agriculture in the area. "Of course, for many years, tobacco was the primary crop in the county, but even then, we advocated diversification, and many farmers did expand their livestock operations as well as their field crops," McCullen says.

One of the most significant achievements of McCullen's term as extension agent was the establishment of the North Carolina Tobacco Growers Association. The organization had its beginning in Columbus County, and McCullen was a key figure in getting it organized and in helping it become a major state organization.

"So much has changed in agriculture and in the way that the extension service delivers its service," McCullen says. "Technology is now a major factor not only in how farmers learn about advances and changes in production and marketing, but it is also a major factor in how they produce their crops."

He continues: "Of course, one of the major changes is the decrease in the number of 'family farms.' To be competitive and more productive, farmers have had to increase the size of their operations, and that has necessitated an increase in technology and, most importantly, the knowledge of how to use that technology. Farmers now have to be more educated about changes in production and marketing, and in many cases, the best way to utilize those changes is to also adopt a corporate operating structure."

Although McCullen can make those observations outside the extension service, he still is involved in agriculture. For the past twenty-seven years, he has been growing Christmas trees and strawberries—still a man of the soil. But he also finds time to travel. Even then, that old work ethic played a part. He and his wife, Lois, have taken their camper to Yellowstone Park, but not just as visitors. They got a job with one of the hotels there and toured the area during their time off. They did the same thing at Dollywood in Tennessee, where they were employed as part of the county fair area of the park.

At eighty years old, Garland McCullen is not slowing down. He and Lois still live on the lake that attracted him to the area in the first place. Their two sons, Dan and Newlyn, and their families live close by and they get in their camper and travel "when the notion strikes" them. Garland McCullen has not only been an agricultural extension agent but life extension agent as well.

J.D. Peterson: Man of Many Talents

Back when tobacco was king, the castle was an old building where the sticky green weed was turned into marketable golden leaves. There was certainly nothing royal looking about those barns—no spires or parapets. They were simple structures, usually wooden with a tin roof and a shed on at least one side. It wasn't the building that created the alchemy; it was the fire inside, a flame fed by wood cut from the surrounding forests and fed into an incinerator with flues that encircled the floor of the barn. The curing process necessitated constant attention to create just the right amount of heat at the right time. There was someone at the barn all day and night, feeding the fire or adjusting ventilation. It was time-consuming, back-breaking work.

Then along came a fellow named J.D. Peterson. He didn't look like royalty, but he had a tremendous influence on the tobacco industry that was so much a part of the lives of the kingdom. In November 1946, J.D. drove to Washington, DC, to register his new invention with the US Patent office. He drove there to personally show the drawing to "whoever needed to see it." What he presented to the patent office was a design for an oil-burning tobacco curing system. The patent number was 2512964. It would change tobacco farming and, consequently, the lives of hundreds of families that depended on the crop to make their livelihood. The kingdom had a prince.

This man who had such an influence on the kingdom of tobacco was not of royal lineage. He grew up in Slap Swamp, an area near Wannanish, a town within the town of Lake Waccamaw. When he was about ten years old, his family moved to Wilmington, where he immediately went to work delivering the *Wilmington Star* newspaper and doing other odd jobs.

When he was twelve (long before child labor laws), he began an apprenticeship at Hanover Iron Works while going to school at night. But he never finished his formal education. At age thirteen, he took his newly acquired skills to the "big paying jobs up north." Because of his skills and the fact that he looked much older than his age, he found employment, but before he did, he wrote his mother a letter to tell her how well things were going for him. He later admitted that he might have exaggerated his status. He bought a stamp with his last pennies to mail that letter, then retired for the night in a cardboard box on the street in Steubenville, Ohio. He soon found employment and moved into a boarding house.

His job was working on high-rise bridges and buildings that utilized his welding skills. To earn a little extra money, usually a quarter, he would dive off a bridge to retrieve a tool that he or one of his co-workers had dropped into the water.

Like so many other native Southerners, the cold northern winters encouraged him to move back to warmer climates and the developing construction boom in Florida. Most of the roads were still unpaved, and the hot sand would cause innumerable flat tires. "It took a while to get to Florida," he said.

North Carolina kept calling him back home, so he returned to Fayetteville, where he opened a speakeasy at a time when the sale of alcohol was illegal. This necessitated numerous trips to the mountains to obtain the liquor for his business. Occasionally, he would have "brief contact" with law enforcement, including some fleeing down dirt roads at night.

He soon gave up the bar business and, in 1938, came back home to Columbus County, where he entered the welding and construction business. He had begun putting a slate roof on the courthouse when he noticed a young lady in a red suit and black pumps with a matching handbag walking from the hospital toward downtown for some shopping. J.D. rushed down to offer her a ride. The lady was Lillian Squires.

J.D. jokingly told his version of the meeting. According to J.D., Lillian walked around that courthouse in "that little red suit" until he got dizzy watching and had to come down. In any case, sometime later they were married, a union that lasted fifty-eight years.

It is unclear exactly what attracted J.D.'s interest in tobacco curers, but he began building metal flues to use in wood-burning tobacco barns. He was always looking for ways to improve his product. At that time, adjusting the temperature as part of the curing process involved going into the heated barn. J.D. discovered that heating the barn with oil (kerosene) would allow the management of the heat (regulating the amount of fuel) to be done by using a carburetor and a steel burner. Combining this with the metal flues he already was making was a part of the process of developing the new curing system.

Then, on a fateful winter's day in 1950, J.D. Peterson, a man with only a basic formal education but a creative superior intelligence, drove to the patent office in Washington, DC, to acquire the patent for his new invention.

With word of mouth being J.D.'s primary marketing tool, his Peterson Tobacco Curer began to sell all through the tobacco belt. Although he had some distributors, he sold most of his curers directly to farmers who came to the plant to get the curer. He and his family later moved from Lake Waccamaw to his wife's family farm on the outskirts of Bolton. From there, he expanded his tobacco-curer business to include tin smithing, roofing, and some farming of tobacco, corn, soybeans, and peanuts, as well as raising a few cattle.

Folks who remember J.D. Peterson recall him as a man "who had wide-ranging interests and a mind to match." Sometime in the 1960s, he developed an interest in horses. The primary stimulant for J.D.'s interest in horses came from a horse he gave to his daughter for Christmas. "Daddy had a midlife crisis. He fell in love with horses. He read every book he could put his hands on," says his daughter Vivian.

Just as J.D. had been absorbed in developing the tobacco curer, so did he involve himself in the horse business. One of his first efforts was to train a beautiful Appaloosa mare to stand quietly while J.D. fired a shotgun sitting on the horse's back. They became deer-hunting companions, and knowledge of J.D.'s ability to train horses spread as he successfully worked with other people's mounts.

Horse shows popped up in pastures where enthusiasts would build big round fences and have weekend horse shows, almost informal affairs that involved all ages. J.D.'s show ring was extremely popular as the area's interest in horses grew. As with all his efforts, J.D. placed his own unique stamp on the arena he built at Bolton. His engineering instinct and the observation of muddy arenas elsewhere caused him to build a pond in the middle of the show ring. The result was that even after a heavy rain, shows could be held. Most of the events were "game shows," like barrel racing, pole bending, and ring spearing. But he also had pleasure classes and reining and English classes. People came from all over eastern North Carolina to show and play. Vivian remembered, "Those were fun times!"

In addition to the shows and horse training, J.D. partnered with Sara Sledge, who ran the Ambassador Camp at Lake Waccamaw. He hosted members of the summer camp for riding lessons. Over the years, those sessions would become fond memories for the campers, and succeeding generations would pass greetings from their parents to J.D. as the younger campers created their own memories.

Looking back at accomplishments might be like looking at mirrors facing each other. It is an endless reflection. That is the case with J.D.

Peterson. There is so much to see, and each time we look, there is more to see. But looking at his life is more like looking back through a reflecting kaleidoscope: so colorful, so different, so unique.

The Woman Behind the Man

There is an old axiom that applies to the life of J.D. Peterson: "Behind every great man is a great woman." That certainly applies to J.D. In recounting some of his early years and those that came after he met Miss Lillian (as everyone called her), it would be safe to say that she probably was the catalyst that changed him from the unfocused young adventurer to a man whose vision, creativity, and intelligence changed not only the tobacco industry but also the culture of the area.

Miss Lillian had a deep religious faith, probably a major factor in J.D.'s transformation. She and J.D. married February 18, 1939, when the country was on the brink of war and the future was uncertain. But faith and perseverance prevailed.

Vivian Brown is the youngest daughter of J.D. and Lillian and the only one of three sisters still living. Her recollection of her mother's life is a picture of a unique lady, a woman who was ahead of her time yet, in many ways, exhibited those elements of Southern womanhood that are so much a part of "who we were."

"My mother was born to Leta Blue Squires and Peyton Squires on September 5, 1918. She grew up surrounded by parents and several loving aunts," Vivian says. Miss Lillian, her mother and father, several siblings, and her maternal aunts all lived in the Blue family home near Bolton.

Miss Lillian's story is best told by her daughter Vivian:

[My mother] graduated from Hallsboro High School and attended Flora McDonald College in Red Springs, North Carolina. Her college studies were interrupted by the sudden illness of her mother. Much of the family finances were drained by the illness and death of her mother. She found she could not return to Flora McDonald, so she changed her career path to accommodate what she saw available in Columbus County. There was a severe need for trained nurses in the county, so she entered the nursing program at Columbus County Hospital under the direction of Dr. Edwin Miller. Dr. Miller was a tall man. Mother was short [and] she had to stand on her tiptoes to reach the operating table height to assist in surgeries. When the good doctor noticed this, he made a stool for her to use during surgeries. Mother never forgot the kindness.

On January 19, 1940, Mama and Daddy were blessed with the first of three daughters. My grandfather Peterson also lived with them for the first twelve years of their marriage until he passed away. During these years, [Mother] was caregiver to [her] elderly aunts, who lived just down the road, and Granddaddy Peterson along with her husband and three girls. She was also bookkeeper for Daddy's business. Somehow, she found time to be active in the church where she taught Sunday school.

Although Mother never received her nursing degree, her passion for helping those in poor health continued. When there was sickness or death within a neighbor's family, she was always there to help. At a time when most folks were intimidated by taking insulin or even iron shots, she went back and forth to those homes like a "county nurse," giving injections and helping people understand health principles, which many country folks were hesitant to embrace.

A Mr. Hux from Whiteville organized a radio program on WENC, which was broadcast every Sunday morning at 8:00 a.m. Mr. Hux asked several people in the county to take turns teaching Sunday school from the lesson study quarterly. Mother was one of those people. She was dedicated to this program. I remember, before Mother got her driver's license, the whole family would be up before breakfast, be dressed for church, and be at the radio station in Whiteville before 8:00 a.m. Then we would watch through a large plate glass window as she delivered the lesson over the air. The program was called "Sunday School of the Air."

Throughout my childhood, there were several individuals who came and went in our household simply because they needed a temporary place to live. Mother would provide one for them.

This account may sound like she was an absolute saint. She wasn't! But she was an example to all who were close to her as to how to love and give of yourself to a cause you believe in. She was always on the side of what she saw as "just and right." She never hesitated to stand up with the little guy.

She was a wonderful Christian wife, mother, grandmother, and friend to all. If she had an enemy, they certainly kept to themselves. She had a plaque on the wall in her kitchen which read, "Let me live in a house by the side of the road and be a friend to all." I believe that is exactly what her life exhibited.

Thank you, Vivian, for your wonderful perspective.

Jane Smith Patterson: Modern Communicator

Jane Smith Patterson could read when she was just three years old, and she hasn't stopped since. Her parents encouraged their little girl to pursue with vigor everything and anything that interested her. She was interested in a wide variety of things but particularly liked math and science. That interest gave her a unique background for the role she was to fill as the computer age dawned and grew to become a primary element in the world.

She was only sixteen years old when she graduated at the top of her class at Tabor City High School in 1959, then went on to the University of North Carolina at Greensboro before transferring to the university at Chapel Hill. It was there that she found so many kindred spirits, young people who optimistically thought they could change the world. "I met my first husband at a protest rally. We discovered we had a lot in common, and love grew from there," she says.

They, along with hundreds of others at the university, protested against social injustice in its many forms and gleaned new knowledge that allowed them to broaden their horizons, as well as to seek new answers and create a new world based on technology and a different perspective on what they could accomplish. She graduated from the School of International Studies with a degree in political science. Later, she went on to do postgraduate work at NC State University and additional studies at Harvard University.

Patterson took all that and added her own unique abilities in cooperation with like-minded people. She worked through Governor Jim Hunt's administration first as NC Secretary of Administration, then as Chief Advisor for Policy, Budget, and Technology. She also served as senior adviser for Science and Technology and NC Director of the Office of Technology.

She had previously worked with Governor Dan Moore. "Governor Moore was my mentor," she says. "I learned how government works, and that helped me in every area of endeavor. He taught me that government can change things."

Patterson did change things. She helped develop Univac (Universal Automatic Computer), the first commercially produced digital computer. While working for Governor Hunt, she was instrumental in getting the state government involved in digital and internet technology, including the development of an information highway that connected government with every school district in the state.

In 1991, Patterson created a vice chancellorship of public service and education for the University of North Carolina at Wilmington and served as interim director for advancement.

For twelve years, beginning in 2000, Patterson served as the executive director of the North Carolina Authority, where she developed a program to see that broadband internet was deployed and adopted and that programs for mapping and funding were available to citizen households and businesses across the state.

During her work in government and technology, Patterson has maintained her involvement in social causes. She has campaigned for women's rights in government. Since her early years, she has been involved in the national and state Women's Political Caucus and has crusaded for the Equal Rights Amendment.

For the past eight years, Patterson has been the president of Jane Patterson and Associates in Raleigh. Building on her vast experience with technology and government, she has provided information technology and broadband deployment, adoption, and use to companies in this country and abroad. She also provides consulting service on technology-based economic development.

Patterson credits much of her success to her beginning in Tabor City. "First of all, I came from a family of educators who encouraged me at every turn. I had wonderful teachers, and I made lifelong friends there."

Patterson is a true activist who takes on challenges where and when she sees them and pursues the challenge with an enthusiasm and commitment that gets results.

There is an old English proverb that could apply to Jane Smith Patterson: "Great oaks from little acorns grow."

JOHN WILSON: GIVING BACK

When John Wilson was growing up in southeastern North Carolina, there wasn't a public tennis court within thirty miles of his home. He was born in Elizabethtown, lived awhile in Whiteville, and finally moved to Bolton. He never thought about the game of tennis. He played a little basketball at Armour High School, where he graduated, but participation in that sport faded with age.

So how did he get to be a professional tennis referee?

"I like tennis because it is not always a team sport. If I win or lose, it is my loss or my win. And it is something I can do even as I get older," he replied.

Wilson didn't play his first tennis match until he moved to Springfield, Massachusetts, after a stint in the army. He was already twenty-three years old. There, he met one of his brother's friends who gave him a racket that had been relegated to the trunk of his car. That led to his one and only tennis lesson.

"We played a lot on weekends, sometimes all day long. It finally got to where I wanted to play in local tournaments, and I was getting pretty good," Wilson says. "I started playing in the USTA [United States Tennis Association] and was on a New England team that won a national championship in Key Biscayne, Florida, in 1989."

His friend who had given him the tennis racket also introduced him to refereeing tennis. Following his friend's encouragement, Wilson attended a clinic in Connecticut and became an official in 1996.

"I started out refereeing high school matches and junior tournaments. My first professional match was as a line official with Bill Barber in Cape Cod, Massachusetts," he recalls.

Wilson has been a referee for national junior events and college matches, including all Atlantic Coast Conference schools and most of the Ivy League schools, and four World Tour matches as a professional line coach.

With a touch of appropriate pride, Wilson says, "I was very pleased to be selected for the US Open Finals in 2017, and [it was] a real honor [to win] the Fed Cup and the Davis Cup in 2018."

Even with the impressive list of professional events in his background, Wilson looks back at his work with developing young players as his most important accomplishment. He helped get a junior program started back in Springfield that has seen hundreds of young adults not only become good tennis players but also use their involvement with the game to find the confidence they need to help them overcome challenges and reach goals they never dreamed of.

The program is called NetSet Jr. and has been an integral part of Wilson's life. Paul Bolte, division manager of United Parcel Service in Springfield and John's immediate supervisor, says, "John not only teaches the game; he teaches them about life. He stresses the value of a good education and playing it straight by avoiding drugs and trouble and keeping your life focused on a larger goal. John is their role model. He's proud of this fact yet is very humble."

When asked why he devotes so much time to this, Wilson says, "I haven't forgotten where I came from."

Many of John's players have gone on to college and have used tennis as a tool to succeed. "The NetSet system illustrates the success a true grassroots effort can have," Wilson says. "As long as someone gets a program started, youngsters who might not otherwise play tennis will be introduced to the game. Some will become highly skilled, and then those who were once beginners can keep the program going by becoming instructors, and everyone involved can keep playing regardless of their level."

In addition to the benefits of playing the game, NetSet, under Wilson's guidance and effort, has provided scholarships to many inner-city youths who were able to continue their education because of the financial assistance. Wilson's fundraising includes a major junior tournament in Springfield, as well as seeking support from corporations and foundations—particularly those related to the tennis profession.

After her first year at Spellman College in Atlanta, Jennifer, a scholarship recipient, wrote John: "I have a current semester GPA of 3.0 and am on the honor roll. I hope to continue my tennis playing next year."

Sabrina wrote: "My family and I thank NetSet for the generous contribution towards my education. Without the support of your organization, I could not afford to attend a prestigious school like Columbia University."

These scholarships were not athletic scholarships but were given based on need and character.

"And I enjoyed the college involvement, as well. It is really gratifying to see players growing into the sport and representing their respective schools," Wilson says. "When I see a former college player on the pro tour, it makes me feel like I might have played a part in his success."

In reflecting on his illustrious career, he says, "I am very fortunate to be able to stay in the game after my playing days are over." Wistfully, he adds, "I really believe if I had started playing tennis at an early age, I could have competed in Ashe Stadium [Arthur Ashe Stadium, the largest tennis stadium in the world]." Recalling standing in that august venue, he says, "When you're in Ashe Stadium, there is so much magic in the air, especially when current and future Hall of Fame players are on the court."

Wilson is surprisingly candid about commenting on some of those professional players with whom he has shared the court. "Serena Williams is the greatest female athlete I've ever met. She is phenomenal," he says.

As a referee, what does he think about the relatively new attitude of sportsmanship involving some of the professional players? "They are just jerks," he says.

What does he think has changed the perception of tennis from the ultimate game of sportsmanship to the frequent site of player temper tantrums? "Money. There is a lot of difference in reacting to a call when you only lose a point as compared to losing a million dollars," he observes.

Wilson gets back home more often now and is interested in possibly developing a professional team in the Wilmington area. "After all, this is the home of Althea Gibson. What greater tribute to her than to have a professional team in her hometown?" he says.

A more immediate goal is to create a Wilmington replica of her statue that now stands in front of Ashe Stadium. But maybe there should be a statue of John Wilson too.

MYRA SHIRD: PROBLEM SOLVER

Myra Shird is always looking for trouble. She doesn't go around creating it; she goes around finding ways to solve situations that created trouble and were created by trouble. In fact, it's her job to look for troubles such as hurricanes, tornadoes, floods, droughts, fires and, sometimes, pandemics. She works for the Federal Emergency Management Agency [FEMA], the folks everyone looks for when disaster strikes.

Myra is a Whiteville native and a graduate in the 1983 class of Whiteville High School. She was an excellent student in high school—a scholar, popular with her classmates, a member of the student council, and a cheerleader. It would probably be no surprise to those who knew the outgoing young lady that she would pursue a career involving communication. Every professional problem solver must place communication as the primary tool in defining and solving difficulties.

So naturally, she chose to attend one of the best communications schools in the country (in my humble personal opinion)—the University of North Carolina at Chapel Hill. She earned a bachelor's degree in a field that involved a wide range of communication skills: radio, television, and motion pictures. (This area of study would later be combined with other departments within the school of journalism to create a BA in communication studies.)

Eight years later, Myra got a specialized master's degree in rhetoric from San Diego State University before coming back to North Carolina to pursue and receive her Ph.D. in 2001 from the University of North Carolina at Greensboro while teaching at North Carolina Agricultural and Technological State University. She designed and was chair of the Speech Communication Studies department while at NC A&T.

Probably one of the most important programs Myra became involved with was Harvard University's National Preparedness Leadership Initiative. The project "combines conceptual rigor with pragmatic insights developed through faculty research on events" including Hurricane Katrina, the Boston Marathon Bombing, and infectious disease outbreaks. It integrates applied neuroscience, game theory, psychology, group dynamics, and more practical tools and techniques to improve leadership effectiveness.[1] Essentially, the program takes an intensive look at the past to learn how to better prepare and react to the future.

So what was Myra going to do with all this education? She began to pass it on to individuals and communities where disaster had made it necessary to reassess community planning in every aspect—organizationally and physically. Her conduit for the application of her knowledge was FEMA. Her job was and is to go to disaster sites and help determine the damage, assess the needs, provide guidance to the community, ascertain resources, and find other ways to not only rebuild but also create a better environment than existed prior to the disaster.

FEMA is a federal program under the supervision of the US Department of Homeland Security. Part of the program function is to provide funds, but just as important, it's intended to help the community become better prepared should another disaster strike.

Having grown up here on the Carolina coast, Myra knows firsthand the effect of hurricanes. She combines that understanding of not only small rural areas but also the expanded disaster of urban areas. Whatever

---

1 "The National Preparedness Leadership Initiative," Crisis Response Journal, accessed May 31, 2023, https://crisis-response.com/Articles/612297/The_National_Preparedness.aspx.

the disaster is, whether it be a hurricane, tornado, flood, drought, a giant freeze, or a wildfire, the damage can change the whole community.

"What I do now is a way to use all my skills," she says. "I want to not only help people reclaim their communities but to also re-envision themselves, to not just build back but build back better than it was before disaster struck."

Of course, FEMA decides where it sends her, and sometimes that assignment may take as long as fifty weeks. In that amount of time, Myra becomes more than an observer and more than a consultant; she becomes part of the community she is helping.

"The hardest part of my job is coordinating all the organizations involved in the effort to make sure we are all headed in the same direction and not becoming counterproductive," she says.

However, even with the connection she made with the communities she serves and the continuing commitment to helping people wherever she will be sent, there's no place like home. For the past several years, Myra had lived in Greensboro and Washington, DC, among other places, but it wasn't home. When she recently returned to Whiteville to attend her mother's funeral, she realized that with modern mobility and communication, she could live anywhere. What better place to live than where she grew up, with family connections and old friends close by? She even has her horse here. "Now I'm home!" she says. "I love small towns. I want to get involved here," she adds with that excitement that only comes with optimism for the future.

Growing up in Whiteville, Myra Shird certainly had dreams of expanding her horizons, getting a good education, and being "successful." She probably never dreamed that her life would take on the dimensions it has: the opportunity to learn not only more about how to communicate with people but how to help them better communicate with each other to overcome seemingly insurmountable obstacles and, in the process, have a positive effect on millions of lives. She has offered hope to the hopeless, cast a light in the shadow of disaster. She has traveled around the world; met and worked with extremely talented, knowledgeable, often famous and influential people; helped to rebuild that which had been destroyed; and create in its place, one community at a time, a world safer than she found it.

Quite an accomplishment for a little girl from Whiteville. And she's not finished yet.

Imagine Mama's House

We sold Mama's house a little while back just before she died. We realized she wasn't coming back from the nursing home, and she told us to sell it. So, as always, we did what Mama told us to do.

Of course, I miss the house. It's where I grew up. It held all those memories of family and friends that made up my life for almost twenty years. But it has also released those memories now to run rampant through my mind and pop up unexpectedly. It is right next door to the Hallsboro Baptist Church, which I still attend, so I see the house at least once a week. And as I walk from the parking lot to the church, I can't help looking at the old house. I try not to get too sentimental about it. Good folks live there now, and frankly, it only takes a minute to walk across the parking lot, so I don't have a lot of time to think about the past right then.

But sometimes when I'm driving through rural North and South Carolina, I'll see something that will make me think of the little house in Hallsboro back in a different time. The late 1940s and the 1950s were great years for most of us. A world war had ended, family members had come home from fighting in places we had never heard of before the war, and prosperity was knocking on every door.

A surefire trigger for memories is a dirt road. Admittedly, I don't travel on them much anymore, mainly because there aren't many left. I was coming home from Southport the other day and took a voluntary detour down a dirt road I hadn't been on in a long time. It had rained just enough to settle the dust and not create a boggy mess. Driving on a dirt road that wasn't dusty made me think of Mama's house. I remember Mama fussing about all the dust that arose from the road in front of the house. There was not a lot of traffic on the road, about as many mules and wagons as automobiles, but to Mama, each car intentionally created dust that would seek out the open windows during the hot summer days and settle on her furniture. One of my first chores was dusting furniture.

When I was thinking about writing this story, I called the Department of Transportation in Whiteville to find out when the Hallsboro road was first paved. Kenneth Clark, the district engineer for the NC Division of Highways, kindly looked it up and gave me a history of the road. It was not until about 1955 that the whole road was paved with asphalt. Other substances had been used but not what we now call permanent pavement.

There were plenty of children in Hallsboro back then, and me and my sister Linda's closest playmates lived just on the other side of the churchyard from our house. Bernice Ray resided on the corner of the dirt street, and Paul and Maude Wyche lived in the house beside her. They later moved to a bigger house just through the woods behind our house. There was no Parks and Recreation department in Hallsboro then—nor is there now—but the churchyard was big and grassy and had a dirt driveway and a few spindly young cedar trees. That was our playground. We made up games to fit the number of people in the churchyard.

A few years ago, the church underwent significant repairs, and several softballs, baseballs, footballs, round rubber balls of various sizes, remnants of kites, and other similar items were recovered from the crevices of the church roof.

Our house was the next to the last house before you left Hallsboro going north. My Aunt Lucille lived in the last house right beside ours. Past her house were woods and ditches and a dirt road, a kind of extension of our playground. As I was driving down the dirt road coming from Southport, I saw two boys squatting down next to a ditch that ran off into the woods from the dirt road. I don't know what they were doing, but sometimes Paul and I would look for crawfish in the ditches. We probably found some, but I don't know what we did with them. I'm pretty sure we didn't eat them. We'd find minnows in a pool in one of the ditches, take them home, nurture them, and then give them full burial rites the next day.

For folks who lived through the tragedy, there are not very many good memories of Hurricane Hazel that hit the area in 1954. But for my playmates and me in Hallsboro, Hurricane Hazel added to our recreation area by creating some of the most elaborate "forts" and "camps" you can imagine. Picture large oak trees and pine trees slain by the hurricane, the giant roots coated with mud, and the fallen treetops forming ladders parallel to the ground. When the mud dried, it created an abundance of ammunition for dirt fights between the fallen forts.

As I write this, I realize I haven't written anything about Mama's house except its location. Maybe it's because growing up in a small rural town in the South in the middle of the twentieth century was a great time to be alive, a story all its own. Maybe it's because the house was just one part of the great adventure we created with our imaginations.

Imagine that—dust and all.

The Good Around Me

Most of this book was written during the COVID-19 pandemic. The pandemic affected every part of the world, even my little small-town world. So I had to mention it, but I chose not to dwell on it. Instead, I have chosen to write about other times and places that recall more pleasant circumstances. Maintaining that perspective of looking back instead of at the current situation has not been easy. In the past, if I had seen a lot of people wearing masks, I would have assumed they were up to something, probably an activity in which they didn't want to be recognized.

If I had walked into the grocery store and seen people making a conscious effort to stay at least six feet away from me, it would have hurt my feelings to be shunned by people I thought were friends.

If I had walked down the aisles of that store and noted the complete absence of toilet paper, I would have wondered if somebody had put a laxative in the city water tank.

I would have questioned my eyesight and my sanity as I saw a line of folks outside the liquor store and the church doors locked.

So, as I've written this book, instead of looking at the current situation, at all the changes that had occurred, I have endeavored to try to look at the positive aspects of the world around me, particularly those things that have not changed.

Fortunately, the lawn mower repair business was one of those things that remained, being designated as "essential" when we went into quarantine, and I was able to get my lawn mower back in running condition. After I mowed the lawn, I sat down in the shade of a crepe myrtle tree and smelled that new mown grass mixed with the aroma of the steak my wife was cooking on the grill.

I looked across the backyard at the azaleas in full bloom, at the roses climbing up the lattice fence and the wisteria winding its purple flowers around the pine tree.

I watched a family of cardinals (birds, not priests) flitter from one bird feeder to another, causing the wrens and mockingbirds to scatter and search for their food elsewhere.

As the cooling breeze blew under the crepe myrtle, I looked at the big billowing clouds off toward the ocean. I wondered how it would feel if we could walk on clouds. I could see all kinds of creatures in the clouds: a sheep and a dog and a big bull. Behind me I heard the tentative rumble of thunder and turned to see the sky begin to darken as a few raindrops began to fall. I chose to stay under the little arbor even as I saw a flash of lightning streak briefly across the gray cloud. What would it be like to hold a bolt of lightning in my hand, to throw it to earth?

I'm just a human; I'll never know.

As the gentle rain began to fall, I saw a rabbit scamper across the lawn back toward his warren in the copse of woods behind me. I wondered if he was alone or if another rabbit or rabbits were waiting to welcome him safely home. I looked around for the birds that had been feeding, but they were gone. Where do birds go when it rains? Do they find a big leaf to get under or just stay outside and get a bird bath?

The brief shower abated, but the gray clouds still hid the sun. The little crepe myrtle shelter had not kept the rain from getting me wet. I didn't mind. Something about getting wet by the rain makes me feel like I'm a part of the earth, just like the rabbits and birds.

The sky began to brighten just a little, but still I saw no sun. I really was expecting to see a rainbow, but I remembered my grandmother telling me once that there's not always a rainbow after every rain.

Sometimes all you get is the rain.

I started back toward the house. The grass was wet and so were my boots. It occurred to me that I hadn't walked barefoot in a long time. So I took off my boots and walked across the newly mown, wet grass. It felt good. It felt natural.

When I got to the porch, my wife informed me that I would have to take off my wet, dirty clothes before I could come in the house. So as I proceeded to disrobe, I realized that for almost a whole afternoon, I had not thought about coronavirus or any other illness or catastrophe. I had been absorbed by the world around me, the good things, the positive things. That was the perspective I wanted to keep, a look at those verities, those everyday things that never change, the good around me.

No, the rainbow didn't come out this time. But the sun will come out tomorrow.

Adapting for Tradition

There are few things as binding as tradition. It intimates a permanence, the assurance that some things always will be here despite conditions that change all around—businesses, families, things that make up communities. Recent events, particularly the COVID-19 pandemic, have caused so many traditions to be tested, and in fact, some traditions had to yield to the threat of contagion and to the possibility of folks causing harm to each other. It would take something like the COVID-19 pandemic to change the staging of turkey shoots as a part of the Thanksgiving and Christmas holidays in Columbus County.

Persistence prevailed, and several turkey shoots were held in the county anyway. Most are sponsored by volunteer fire departments and other organizations as fundraisers to help meet the needs of that organization. But when asked why they have come out to this event, many had another reason. Dwight Britt and several of his friends traveled from Robeson County to the event in Evergreen.

"It's something to do, and we get out from being shut up with this virus stuff," he says.

"This virus stuff" is taken very seriously by the sponsoring organizations. Participants wear masks, some of which are provided by the organization. They also maintain social distance, and there is a container of hand sanitizer on the same table where the guns are placed.

Plus, the whole event is held outdoors. On one of the nights at the Evergreen shoot, a crisp breeze blows, adding a chill to the air, as well as some additional protection from airborne contaminants.

Several folks show up at the shoot to get the famous steaks cooked on the outdoor grill by fireman Robert Floyd and others. "Steak supper, beautiful night, a little target practice, and a little socializing," is the reason some folks give for coming out to the event.

Turkey shoots are events that have been a part of rural America, particularly in the South, for centuries. The modern activity has changed considerably from its roots. Actually, no turkeys get shot. In fact, the only turkeys around are frozen and given as prizes along with hams and bacon.

The shooter's goal is to fire a shotgun at a paper target placed at some distance and hope that one of the pellets comes closer to the center than the pellets of his competitors. Some folks bring their own weapons, but most use those provided by the sponsors. Although there is much friendly rivalry among the contestants, even the experts admit there is a certain amount of luck involved related to the pattern of the shot.

The contest is divided into groups, and there are seldom many people at the site at any one time. "One night we had about fifty people all together," says Max Hood, a fire department member who has handed out masks and helped to coordinate tonight's shoot. The event is held during the Thanksgiving and Christmas holidays so that over that period of time, even small groups can generate significant revenue. The result of the turkey shoot is to provide some community tradition and raise money to support the fire department and increase the safety of the community.

On this Saturday night, the moon is full and the sky is clear, and a visitor can see clearly the turkey-shoot site sitting in a field amid grain bins, a brightly lit shelter over the cooking area, and a little smoke coming from the cooker. Amid the sounds of the shots fired toward the paper targets is a continuous hum of voices and laughter. These are the sights and sounds of tradition adjusting to a challenge.

Caring for Blind Chickens

At a time when compassion seems to be a rarity, you can find an abundance of it at the north end of Red Hill Road here in Columbus County.

Susan Aycock is a doctor; compassion is a part of her nature. So it should be no surprise then that she would reach out to help *all* creatures great and small, not just humans. That sympathy automatically transferred to two baby chicks born into the flock she keeps at her house.

"I knew there was something neurologically wrong when they kept twirling around and generally seemed disoriented and agitated, but Jack actually diagnosed the blindness," she says, referring to her husband, Jack Johnson. Susan took the chicks under her wing and made sure they were fed and watered and even personally placed them in the hen house to roost at night with the other chickens.

Although Dr. Aycock doesn't name every chick born into her brood, she did give these two special ones names. Ray-Ray is the rooster and Molly is the hen. They are aware of each other and get agitated when they are separated. Although they have a small pen in which they are fed and watered apart from the other chickens, they also are sometimes left outside to roam with the flock.

"Molly has a distinctive chirp we can follow if we need to look for her, and sometimes our dog, Cookie, will find them. We have a sort of peaceable kingdom here," Aycock says. When the two blind chicks are let out into the yard, they are accepted as a part of the flock. "The other chickens don't pick on them. Some of the other roosters may irritate Ray-Ray, but it's just playing rather than harassment," she says.

Aycock doesn't give them any special feed. "They can't eat bread, because not only can they not see it, but the bread is so soft they can't use their beaks to pick it up," she says.

In answer to the question as to what was to become of the chicks as they grew older, Aycock says, "We'll continue to take care of them as long as we need to, but we would hope to find a home for them as a pair. We don't want to separate them. They would make excellent companions. They like to be held. It calms them, and I think they do have a sense of security with people who care for them."

Colonel Sanders is not in their future.

DONNA SPIVEY: IN THE MIDDLE OF IT ALL

When you walk into Donna's Fine Instruments Plus in Chadbourn, you immediately are confronted by walls and every floor area covered with musical instruments. There are records too. You remember those circular vinyl discs that we used to play on record players?

And two rooms full of photographs, some signed by music legends like Bill Monroe and Ralph Stanley, along with a plethora of photos of lesser-known musicians. And in the middle of it all is Donna Spivey.

Some bluegrass music fans know her as "The Hickory Hill Songbird" for her many years singing with her band, Hickory Hill Bluegrass. She is still singing like she did when she had the band and like she did when she was seven years old, singing with her father's gospel group on WTAB in Tabor City. She sings because she loves it. And she's good at it. Like every professional, she gets better the more she plays, and in her case, that's often.

Music always has been a part of her life, but it wasn't until 2009 that she got into the sale of musical instruments. For nearly sixty years, A.R. Carter had operated a music store in Chadbourn. He died in 2005, and four years later, Donna made an offer to buy the business from Mrs. Carter. Her response to Donna's offer was, "He would want you to have it." In just four months, the purchase was completed, the store paid for, and Donna had taken another step into the music business.

Going into the retail business didn't take Donna out of performing. She continues to play at music festivals and conventions and a wide variety of venues around the country. But her favorite performances might be right there in the store in Chadbourn. In addition to the regular Friday night open mic sessions in the store, she says, "Sometimes people will be driving through Chadbourn on the way to the beach and see the store and stop in just to see what and who we are. I always greet my customers, and during conversation, I usually ask them if they play an instrument, and if they do, I ask if they would like to play one of my instruments. We have a lot of spontaneous jam sessions right here in the store. And those folks come back again and again. I have made of lot of friends from those jam sessions with folks just passing through."

If you ask Donna what she enjoys most about playing music, particularly bluegrass, she'll tell you, "It just gets my blood to flowing. It's a feeling that I can't explain. I'm sure other people have similar feelings about music, but everybody is different, and every experience I have playing with other people adds to my enjoyment. I love everybody and particularly people who share my passion for music."

Like so many country/bluegrass performers, Donna has spent time in Nashville. She has played in a wide variety of venues in the Capital of Country Music and all around the country: small cafes, large auditoriums, and a lot of recording studios. Many of the hours in recording studios were spent recording songs she wrote. She has recorded over a dozen songs she wrote for other performers.

"I write the music and somebody else writes the lyrics," Donna says. The result is always the classic sound of acoustic instruments that echo the tradition of country and bluegrass. "There is a nostalgia to my music that takes people back to a sound and time that they remember as being good," she adds.

Some music critics have noted a decline in the popularity of bluegrass music over the years, but many of today's commentators see a resurgence of the old genre as sales of the music have been increasing recently.

"People want a break from the bad news and all the negative stuff around us," Donna says. "Bluegrass lifts us up." Part of the reason may be that folks like Donna's friend Kim White up in Marion, Virginia, have brought bluegrass to the public notice with television programs like *Song of the Mountains* on public television every Saturday night. "The more people hear it, the more people like it," Donna says.

One of her favorite places to play is at music festivals held around the country.

"That's where I meet a lot of people who share a love for my kind of music. The informal sessions with fellow musicians occur backstage or even in the shade of the trees surrounding the stage at the festivals. It's fun, always has been, always will be," Donna says with a laugh. "There's a fraternity of musicians that appreciates and perpetuates bluegrass. We got the famous like Bill Monroe, Lester Flatt, and Earl Scruggs, along with the more recent stars like Doyle Lawson and Rhonda Vincent. But some of the most important players in my life have been not so famous but just as good or better at playing. My great granddaddy, Devon Ludlum, down at Old Dock, was one of my early inspirations, and my daddy—J.C. Lewis—and Slim Mims and so many others from right around here have taught me a lot over the years."

Although Donna doesn't have a band right now, she still performs all over the country. As she was being interviewed for this story, she was preparing to go to Carthage, North Carolina, to perform. "Musicians are always looking for a place to play. Even if I don't have my own band, I just make a few phone calls and we got a band," she says.

The world is full of music; it's the universal language. Wherever bluegrass is being played, Donna will be the interpreter right there in the middle of it all.

(Listen to Bill recite this poem, track number 2 on Just Down the Road.*)*

Moonshine Heritage

No headlights shown through the darkness,
only moonlight to guide the way.
They'd deliver their load to Charlottetown
before the light of day.

Somewhere along the darkened trail,
in hiding, waited The Law.
The two would come together
in the greatest race you never saw.

The dust rolled and the sirens wailed
searing the mountain night.
The Chase was on, God turned his head,
'cause neither man was right.

They dueled 'round the curves and hills
and up the mountainside.
The engines roared together
as Death raced side by side.

Somewhere in the darkness
the devil took the hand,
and the revenuer left the mountain
headed for the Promised Land.

The moonshiner headed on down the road,
now a solitary way.
He'd make it into Charlottetown
before the light of day.

In another time and another place
the race would take up again,
a race run with hundreds of cars
driven by driven men.

They'd make more money than he ever got
for all of his moonshine.
But they'd race with a passion shared
as they headed for the finish line.

The men now racing 'round the track
aren't haulin' mountain dew;
they're chasing a dream of fame and fortune
attained by very few.

But each time you sit at that track
and thrill to the race and the crowd,
look up—you'll see that moonshiner
racing through a cloud.

Race on down that mountain road
with the law on your back!
Your spirit lives on today
'round that oval track.

Race on with the dream
of making one more haul,
doing the best you can,
that's all, that's all.

The Last Mules?

There was a time when mules were a familiar sight in the rural South. In fact, mules were a big part of agriculture and transportation in general for much of the history of America. Most historians agree that no less a personage than George Washington had the first mule in America, the result of the mating of Royal Gift, a breeding jack (literally a royal gift from the king of Spain) to a mare at Mount Vernon. There's a good possibility that some of Royal Gift's progeny ended up in Columbus County. However, regardless of such an auspicious heritage, the breed has almost reached the end of the line. As far as can be determined, there are fewer than five or six mules left in the county.

Three of those mules are owned by Dr. Tiffany Barnhill. She has a veterinary practice here in the county and maintains her mules on her farm near Sidney. A visit to Dr. Barnhill's farm belies the oft held opinion that mules are kept in old run-down stables and are somehow lower class than high-stepping show horses. The visitor enters the gated driveway and immediately sees horses grazing in a pasture and paddocks. The driveway ends at the entrance to an indoor training facility with a healthy pasture in front of it. In that pasture are three mules: one male mule and two mare (female) mules. It is quickly apparent that they are well cared for as their coats shine in the spring sun and the manes and tails are clipped and clean. They graze contently, paying little attention to the visitors.

As Dr. Barnhill stands at the fence and calls the names of each mule, they amble toward her. "Come Molly. Come on Jet. Come on Daisy. They think I'm going to feed them," she says. And she does, as they nicker softly and eat grain from her hand.

"They each have their own personality, and I have to admit that Daisy is my favorite," Barnhill says. "She gave me the worst seven months of my life when I first started to train her. Broke my back. But after I figured out how to train her, she became my favorite."

Dr. Barnhill rides her mules on trail rides. "They aren't draft bred. They might plow, but that's not what I use them for. I just enjoy them. I love 'em!" she says.

She has been working with mules for more than twenty years—most of her life. Her love for her mules is evident as she feeds them, rubs them, and talks to them.

"Mules make the best trail-riding animals," Dr. Barnhill says. "They don't go into places they can't get out of. They don't spook easily. They don't get tired as quickly as horses because they are not excitable, and they are comfortable to ride. They don't overeat, so they hardly ever founder. Mules have a reputation for being stubborn, but that's not so. They just have strong opinions about what they are supposed to do.

"Mules are trained differently than horses too. You can't force a mule to do anything. You have to find a way to make him or her think that what you want them to do was their idea."

In response to the question, "How did you become so involved with mules?" Dr. Barnhill says, "I just love 'em. I love mules." A visitor might think that somewhere on a post or a tree is a heart with "Tiffany Loves Mules" carved in it.

Over the years, mules have transitioned from mostly work animals to recreation animals. There are associations of mule owners that hold trail rides and mule shows. One such show was held at the Boys and Girls Homes arena at Lake Waccamaw in 2005. Mules participate in the same show classes as horses, including English pleasure, reining, and carriage. The jumping classes are a little different. Although there are some regular jumping classes, in a mule show, the rider dismounts and the mule jumps "flat-footed" (from a standing position) over the jump. They call this "coon jumping."

But there was a time when the long-eared equines were a major element in working the fields and woods. They have been replaced by tractors and other modern equipment. At one time, the buying and selling of mules was a major enterprise with at least one sale barn in every town. There are still folks who remember Sam Fuller and Rex Squires's barns in Whiteville, and Mutt Jolly had a barn in Chadbourn. Fuller's barn was located on Madison Street in Whiteville, and Mr. Jolly's barn on Brown Street in Chadbourn. When shipments of mules would come into the railroad station, they would be herded down the street to the barns. It was a common parade, but one that still drew people to watch them make the trip. Now those parades are just memories.

Mules also were sold at the livestock markets, and regular auction sales would be held, as well as individual sales. Springtime was the busiest time at the barns, when farmers would buy and trade mules to be used in preparing and tilling the land from which they made their living. Even in more recent years, some folks would buy a mule to plow in the spring, tend their garden, and then sell the mule in the fall and repeat the process each year. But at the height of their usefulness, mules also were used year round as family transportation. Many a mule that had plowed the fields was brushed and curried before being hitched to the wagon that would take the family to church or to town to buy supplies.

Everybody who has ever owned a mule has a story to tell. As the number of mules declines, the stories will remain, even as new stories are created by folks like Dr. Barnhill.

Southeastern Livestock Auction Company

There is something about a livestock auction that is pure Americana. It is tradition. It is a celebration, a festival of nature complete with the sights and sounds and smells that have been a part of our heritage, our tie to the land, for centuries. Southeastern Livestock Auction in Chadbourn has been a part of that celebration for thirty-eight years. It is appropriately "out in the country" just off Highway 410, south of town. It is a fairly large building, constructed of wood and metal with sturdy pens, so prospective buyers can see what's for sale before taking a closer look on the grounds.

"I've been working at the auction since I was five years old," Buddy McPherson says. He and his wife, Morgan, are the second-generation owners and operators of the market, which was begun by his father, Alfred McPherson. On sale day, they have a total of fourteen people working at the auction.

"We've had the sale every Monday, except for holidays, since we started. We did miss one sale after the old barn burned, but we got right back at it even before we got the barn rebuilt," Buddy says.

Although the auctions are held on Mondays, the work is weeklong. Local sellers often bring the livestock in sometime earlier in the week, and those animals have to be fed and watered. Animals bought by the market for resale also need to be fed. Someone, usually Morgan, must answer hundreds of phone calls while Buddy talks with prospective buyers in markets as far away as Kansas and Nebraska.

Southeastern Livestock is the only livestock auction in southeastern North Carolina. There is one in Sampson County, North Carolina, and another in South Carolina.

"Our customers are the local farmers and what some call 'hobby farmers' who just like being in the livestock business," Buddy says. "These are our neighbors, and we get to know them as friends. We try to accommodate them both in the sale and purchase of the animals."

He also is the auctioneer, so his knowledge of the crowd that gathers for the sale is important in keeping the sale running smoothly. "I can tell who is really interested in what's in the sale ring. I know what he wants, and I keep my eye on him as the bidding progresses. It is all about relationships. We build trust between us and the buyers and sellers. They know we aren't going to misrepresent what is being sold. Sellers know that they will be paid the day they sell their animals, and buyers know that the animals they buy are healthy and sound. Sometimes the market will buy the stock and feed it or send it to a stockyard before selling it to a processing plant."

Buddy explained how his business works. "We sell livestock, all kinds—hogs, cows, goats, and sometimes some horses or ponies—and on the second Friday of each month, we sell chickens. Most of the sales are to individuals, particularly cattle and hogs. About half the goats go to individuals and half to processing plants. 'Course all the chickens go to individuals, and you'd be surprised at the people who buy the poultry. Sometimes they just buy on impulse and have to go home and make a place to keep 'em!"

The livestock sale usually begins around one in the afternoon, but it is preceded by a tack sale at nine that morning that sells not only tack but just about anything else, including furniture and fly spray.

The festive atmosphere is most evident when Buddy mounts the auctioneer stand above the sale ring. The folks in the audience focus on him and whatever is in the pen. Once he starts his chant, bidders make sometimes almost imperceptible moves to indicate a bid. He usually knows who wants a particular pen of animals, and his eyes move quickly over the crowd. It doesn't take long for the sale to transpire. He brings the auction gavel down, shouts, "Sold to …" and immediately the ring men bring in the next animal or animals.

The audience on a particular day during the pandemic is a cross section of the people of southeastern North Carolina. Some are wearing masks. Chairs have been placed to meet social distancing requirements. It is a hot summer day, and the air in the barn is stirred by fans, but the heat is still there. All ages and races are represented, and there is friendly conversation shared by folks who are regular customers and those who are there for the first time. There is a sense of camaraderie here that is seldom found in today's divided society. Everyone has the same chance to bid, make individual decisions on how much and what they buy, and how much they are willing to pay for it. This is the free enterprise system at its finest.

The Train of Dreams

There are hundreds of salvaged train depots across North Carolina and throughout the rural South. They have been saved from destruction by individuals and groups who have turned them into museums, meeting halls, offices, or in some cases, private residences and a variety of other uses. I'm glad they saved them. I'm particularly proud of the ones we have in Columbus County: Lake Waccamaw, Chadbourn, and Fair Bluff.

For a very long time, railroads were the arteries of commerce. Just about everything we used came to us by rail. Eventually, trucks and airplanes replaced trains in so many areas, and the need for the depots disappeared as the railroad tracks were taken up in some places.

There still exists a real need for trains to transport goods and people. And there is a strong possibility that the need for more trains will increase as the cost of other forms of transportation increases.

In all honesty, I don't know much about the commercial viability of the return of passenger trains or the sustainability of freight trains. I hear and read about the financial struggles of the commuter trains and Amtrak, and I have serious doubts about their ability to stay alive, much less expand. But I wish they would.

For me, a train is not so much about business as it is about a sense of romance that I first felt as a boy when I saw or heard a train come through my little town. Each time a train stopped in Hallsboro, I wondered where it had been and where it was going. To me, the rails weren't just steel beams supporting and guiding giant locomotives. They were magic ribbons that could detach themselves from the earth and cross stormy oceans, steamy jungles, and "'the Frozen North."

As I got older, I pictured myself aboard the Orient Express, which had made a slight detour from eastern Europe to pick me up in Hallsboro. I wondered which of those folks getting on the train were really spies dressed in bib overalls.

There used to be a stretch of railroad that ran east of Hallsboro to Wilmington. There wasn't a bend in the rails. Much of the railroad paralleled the highway, and every time a train came alongside my car as I was headed to Wilmington, I would try to keep it right beside me, windows down, so I could hear the roar of the giant engine and imagine myself at the throttle, racing like Casey Jones to keep on schedule.

Along that same track is the little crossing of Maco, where Joe Baldwin, a conductor on an eastbound train, lost his head one night back in 1897 and, according to legend, is still searching for it. When I was in high school, young folks would make special trips to see Joe's lantern swinging in the night.

When I was growing up, Sam Pierce had the enviable job of meeting each train at Hallsboro to get the mail sack and transport it across the road to the post office. The mail could be put in a wheelbarrow. I spent a lot of time sitting on the depot loading dock waiting for the train bringing me my *Grit* newspapers to be sold door to door every Friday. And I loved talking to Mr. Sam. I learned a lot. I never realized the stories he would tell me would spawn more stories, not only about trains but other parts of my small-town Southern life. Mr. Sam would sit on the loading dock of the train depot and smoke an old bent-stemmed pipe. Years later I took up smoking a pipe. The smell of the tobacco reminded me of Mr. Sam and the stories he told. You might say they were pipe dreams.

In a sawmill town like Hallsboro, life was guided by the sound of whistles—usually the mill whistle. But the sound of the train whistle also regulated our lives. As a small boy, I knew I was supposed to be in bed before the night train came through. Hank Williams wrote in a song once about the midnight train that made him so lonesome he could cry. My train passed well before midnight and made me feel safe and secure.

A short time ago, I spent the night in a hotel in Winston-Salem. I had had a long day talking to folks and was tired when I went to bed. But for some reason, I couldn't go to sleep. I kept going over everything that had happened during the day and reconsidering everything I had said and done.

Then I heard a train. It was a faint sound in the beginning, but it grew louder as it approached. It never came really close, but I could hear the sound clearly. I heard the whistle blow and the sound of the train diminish into the night.

My thoughts drifted to trains rumbling slowly through the jungle and spies dressed in bib overalls—and the small North Carolina town of my youth where they've taken up the railroad tracks.

(Listen to "Small Town Train," track number 10 on Just Down the Road.*)*

A Hundred Fields of Dreams

I have watched the movie *Field of Dreams* more than once. Okay, several times. It is my favorite sports movie. The first sports movie I can remember seeing was *The Babe Ruth Story* with William Bendix as The Babe. I saw that in the old Hallsboro Theater. Bendix played the title role in *The Life of Riley* on television a few years later and kinda took the shine off his Babe Ruth role. I watched *Pride of the Yankees,* the story of the great Lou Gehrig played by Gary Cooper, at school when I was in about the fourth grade.

Sports movies have been a staple of Hollywood for years. And there have been other baseball movies that I have watched more than once: *Major League, Bull Durham, The Natural,* and *A League of Their Own,* the movie about the professional women's league. They were all good.

But *Field of Dreams* was special. It was about more than baseball as a game. It was about people who loved baseball, people like millions of kids who played pickup ball in cow pastures and playgrounds, sometimes in the streets, and some, like me, who played in the churchyards.

There are fields of dreams in every small Southern town. Of all the places I could think of where people would identify with the movie *Field of Dreams,* it would be right here in Columbus County. The role that baseball plays in this county has been documented not only by our local sportswriters but also by national magazines like *Sports Illustrated.* National sports commentators have noted the number of baseball players that have gone (and are still going!) from the ballfields of Columbus County to major and minor league fields all over the country.

As I watched Kevin Costner walk out of that Iowa cornfield onto the major league outfield on television, I knew I was watching a metaphor for so many boys who had made that walk in their dreams. Some of the ballfields in Columbus County have been, and still are, surrounded by fields, if not cornfields then ones growing tobacco and soybeans. There was a time when there was not a solid fence around every field. Sometimes, when there were umpires and coaches, they would set up "field rules," adjustments required because of the condition and/or location that would only apply for that game. Or sometimes the rules came about by mutual agreement.

Some elements of the movie I watched on television made me think of those old ballparks. There was a scoreboard where the numbers were changed by hand; somebody climbed up a ladder and made the change. The outfield fence was wire. I couldn't tell exactly from the television camera if a ball could get caught in the wire. If it had, that would have called for a field rule.

I thought it significant that all the runs scored by both teams resulted from home runs. Did a short outfield make it possible to plant so many baseballs in that cornfield? We used to blame that for a loss at away games.

One of the commentators in the movie said that there were eight thousand corn plants in the field immediately surrounding the ballpark. Who counted 'em? Back here in Columbus County, we may not have known how many stalks of corn or soybean or tobacco plants were in the field surrounding our old ball parks, but we knew who planted 'em.

Some sportswriters and broadcasters might say the movie was a sentimental presentation, a nostalgic look at a game that has become big business, a game now focused on "analytics." Well, it may be for them, but not for me. For me, baseball is still a game, a game in which memories are made and life lessons are learned, a game where grandfathers and fathers and sons can enjoy being together, where they can share memories, cheer on their teams, talk junk to the umpires, and be assured their children and grandchildren can enjoy and share in America's game.

As James Earl Jones said, "It reminds us of all that was good about America and could be good again." I think that fact holds true whether it comes from a major league stadium or a field of dreams in Columbus County.

Is this heaven? No, it's baseball.

Take Me Out to the Ball Game

Last year, my son Will and I continued what I hope will be a tradition. We traveled to Baltimore to watch the Baltimore Orioles and the New York Mets baseball game at the legendary Oriole Field at Camden Yard. The tradition is not to go to Baltimore necessarily, but to go to some major league stadium. Since Will is a big—as in overwhelming—Mets fan, the stadium we travel to will probably be the site of a game between the Mets and anybody else. We plan to go on either his or my birthday. His is in June; mine is in September.

The stadium itself is called Oriole Field. Camden Yard is the site of the old railroad terminal that was torn down to build the stadium in 1994. The historic site is part of the appeal, but the real draw for me is the fact that the field is a throwback to the old baseball venues of the past. Only baseball is played at Oriole Field, so it doesn't change into a football or soccer or polo or any other exhibition field after baseball season. It is just baseball. It was built with tradition in mind.

Will and I almost collectively said, "This is what a baseball stadium is supposed to be." But it wasn't just the uniqueness of that field that appealed to me. Every time I walk into a baseball stadium or sit in the stands of a small-town park, I get that special feeling. The old statement about something being as American as baseball, hot dogs, and apple pie is true. Admittedly, some folks don't think that baseball is "America's game" anymore. The game has taken its licks lately from a focus on multimillion-dollar contracts, drug use, and reports of domestic violence.

But when I go to a baseball game, I put all that stuff aside for just an hour or two.

There is nothing perfect about the boys who play baseball. That's why they are called the "boys of summer." They aren't the millionaires of summer; there is no Adonis of the diamond; there are no saints running the bases. They are *boys* who happen to play for a living. For all the flaws of the game, it is still the pinnacle of every boy's dream when he puts on his first baseball uniform to walk out on the hometown field that someday he will walk out on that big-league field. If the dream is big enough, he'll face a Don Larson and get a hit. He'll slide into home plate under the glove of Yogi Berra and hear the umpire shout, "Safe!" He'll catch a ball on top of the outfield fence to steal a hit from Hank Aaron. (These are old-man heroes.) The young dreamer will hear the roar of the crowd as he rounds the bases, and he'll shuffle his feet and grin when the sportswriters and photographers gather outside the locker room.

And the fans will still forgive him of any baseball sin as long as he gives the game everything he's got. The fans will pay big bucks for a hot dog and Pepsi, sit in the rain, watch the ground crew roll a tarp over the infield, and try to ignore the guy in the stands who disagrees with every umpire call.

Like nearly every boy who grows up in Columbus County, Will started playing Dixie Youth baseball when he was small. Then he played high school and college ball and a little recreational league ball after college. He was a college graduate and a banker before a spring went by when he didn't put on a baseball uniform. So, as we sat in the stands in Baltimore, I asked him how he thought it would feel to walk out on the field for the first time as a player on a major league team. He answered, "Probably like it did when I walked out on the field at Lake Waccamaw for my first Dixie Youth game." It is that sense of excitement that begins every new journey. It is the thrill of "the first time" that can't be duplicated. It is the dream of what may lie ahead, and the only real knowledge you have is that you don't know.

The road that lies ahead for the young dreamer will pass through hundreds of small baseball fields with just two sets of small metal bleachers, parents and grandparents sitting in folding chairs, long trips home after losing a game, big celebrations at McDonald's after a win, an armful of trophies, and enough tears to wet the infield. Most of them won't make it to the big leagues, but they will share that unique thrill of playing America's game long after the lights have gone out and the old glove, like their bones, has stiffened and cracked with age.

That's why it is called America's game in every small town.

A Recollection of Marbles

decided I would clean out my office, a task I had not undertaken for a while, but I was pretty sure I would not discover any bodies in the closet. In the process, I found something from my distant past that did make me smile: a little leather pouch of marbles. It was a tangible sign that I had not lost my marbles. (I know you saw that coming but read on anyway.) There were only a few in the pouch, a remnant of the huge collection I'd once had and a small reminder of my childhood—a time when I would not have been concerned with the recent and ongoing tragedies, even if they'd occurred at the time when those marbles were an active part of my life.

Children have a way of prioritizing the important things in life. To a twelve-year-old boy, winning a game of marbles was far more important than … anything. I believe a child invented the modern game of marbles. No adult could come up with something so simple: little glass balls with all the colorful hues that catch the eye of a child. A game of marbles requires no electricity (batteries or otherwise), and no assembly is required. The rules of the game are not written in three languages on the back of the box they came in. Marbles don't always even come in a box!

The main attraction of marbles is the game itself. Certainly, it is a great game, one of skill and strategy. But a major attraction for me is the marbles themselves. There's something visceral about the smooth feel of the marbles, something about that spherical shape that challenges you. You can't stack marbles without some tangible restraint. Their smoothness makes them elusive. You can't push them together. Their hardness makes them resilient. You can force them against each other, but it is almost impossible to break one marble with another; they just bounce off.

Each marble is unique. I'm sure there may be some marble somewhere that's an exact duplicate of another, but if you look at it long enough, a marble's appearance will change right before your eyes. The shade of color will darken or brighten as the sun's rays strike it. Once you find one that seems to be a genuine one of a kind, that's a keeper. Its value is far above rubies. You don't even put it in the ring for fear it may be taken.

When I was a boy, marbles used to come either in a great big jar or in small bags. They were relatively inexpensive. If you were lucky or looked hard enough, you might run up on a marble that was bigger than the others. That was the shooter. Sometimes, depending on the neighborhood, some guy would come up with a "steelie," a ball bearing gouged out of a piece of wheel found down at the local garage. In some neighborhoods, a steelie was illegal, the legality being determined by a majority of the players. Of course, if the guy who owned the steelie happened to be much bigger than any of the other players, the rule could be waived.

Serious marble players carried their marbles in a small sack (like my leather pouch), or some just kept them in their pocket. That's why marbles had such a unique smell. I know you may wonder who smelled marbles. Well, I did. If you carried around all those marbles in your pocket for a while, they would take on the smell of that pocket. Depending on what else you had in your pocket, the smell could be of apples or oranges or motor oil or the good clean smell of dirt. The smell made them uniquely yours.

Marbles is an old-fashioned game. The origin goes back to Egypt, Greece, and Rome. But the modern adaptation is the result of the development of glass and the availability to children of something different but pretty and simple and cheap. It survived because it adapted to change.

A lot of analogies can be drawn between a game of marbles and the game of life; it is a great temptation to make that comparison. However, consider this: I had a professor in college who taught comparative literature. During a discussion of a novel in class one day, after all of us had given our interpretation of what the author really meant in telling the story, he said, "Your interpretation is correct for you, but sometimes a story is just a story."

Y'all remember that. Sometimes a game is just a game.

A Swamp Legacy

On a hot summer afternoon, I took my grandson, Drew, to visit a cemetery on the edge of Bogue Swamp. It's a family cemetery that dates back to the eighteenth century. According to family history, soldier-ancestors who served in every American conflict from the Revolution through World War II are buried there.

We walked down the dusty road, its two dry ruts dividing the weeds and the still heat simmering over the soybean field on one side and through the stand of planted pine trees on the other.

We were a contrasting pair. Not only am I about two feet taller than my nine-year-old scion, but our attire amplified our generational differences: flip-flops and work boots, shorts and khaki pants, T-shirt and long-sleeved denim shirt with the sleeves rolled up. As the exertion of the walk and the heat of the sun began to take its toll, I realized that my grandson was more appropriately dressed for the trek than I was. The underestimated wisdom of youth?

"How far is it, Granddaddy?"

"Not far. Just a little farther."

"What are those things flying around with the big wings?"

"Dragonflies. We call 'em mosquito hawks. They eat mosquitoes."

"They sure came to the right place to find a meal."

We had sprayed each other down with insect repellant, but that didn't keep the mosquitoes from buzzing around us. We could see them almost swarming just above the weeds in the road.

"Watch out for snakes. All this rain'll make 'em look for high ground."

"The mosquitoes will probably scare them off."

The road began a slight decline, which led us across a small culvert. Water flowed rapidly through the pipe and on down the swamp. "This is called a branch. It's a low place that separates two little higher places."

"Doesn't look very high to me," he replied.

Everything is relative, I thought.

The cemetery was just past the branch. At the entrance was a granite marker: Elbow Pierce Cemetery Circa 1700. A concrete angel stood watch just behind the marker. A stone bench provided temporary repose next to the more permanent resting places. An American flag hung limp in the soggy heat on a metal pole. Behind the angel, spread out beneath the old trees, were the grave markers: some upright slabs of very old marble, a few newer granite headstones, and several wooden markers with only a number on them, the names recorded in a long-lost book.

The cemetery was neat and clean, the result of the annual spring cleaning by descendants of those buried there. There are many such cemeteries in rural areas, respectful repositories for those with no church cemetery available and no funeral home to provide such a place at the time. The annual spring cleaning is a chance for kin to come together, tell old stories, and show respect for the past.

Infant son Born Nov. 1900, Died Dec. 1901 …

Thomas Pierce Co. K 3 NC Arty CSA March 12 1824–Feb 21 1903 …

M. Jay Pierce Co. K 2 Rgt NC Volunteers Sp Am War 1873–1898 …

Infant son and daughter of Alva and Margaret Pierce …

Toward the back of the cemetery was a brick tomb raised about eighteen inches off the ground. A bronze plaque read:

Stephen Smith 1746–1784

Wife Joanna Council 1753–1833

Revolutionary War Soldier

Placed by the descendants D.A.R.

A faded American flag had been placed in the holes of some bricks atop the tomb. Time and weather had almost obliterated the stars and stripes, and the stillness of the swamp gave the scene a dreary appearance.

"I believe Stephen Smith needs a new flag, Granddaddy. You got one back at your house."

"That one at home is way too big. We'll have to go somewhere and find one."

"They probably got one at Walmart or Target. You can get just about anything there."

Even under the shade of the trees, the summer heat seeped through the leaves, and the mosquitoes rose from the grass to greet us with every step we took. It occurred to me that many of the soldiers buried there had endured greater heat and more pestilence than we were suffering, as had many of the others, men and women, who had struggled to build their farms and homes here in the flat, wet land of southeastern North Carolina.

And what was their legacy over three hundred years? They had created a lot or a little; some gained fame and some kept anonymity; some had money, some were poor. All were dead and all were kin. Whatever their legacy, it belonged to an old man and a boy standing in the middle of the swamp cemetery on a hot August afternoon.

(Listen to Bill recite this poem, track number 6 on Just Down the Road.*)*

Keeping the Dream Alive

The two stood on the mountaintop,
the tall mountain made of sand.
The old man felt like Moses
as he gazed into The Promised Land.

They were looking west to the sun,
their backs to the wind and the sea.
And the little girl, his Joshua, asked,
"How are things going to be?"

"I don't really know," he said,
"I can't tell you what to do,
but remember you're tied to the land,
and the land is tied to you.

"What we do with the land God gave us
might not matter to some,
but I want to save it for you children,
and you children yet to come."

Then they walked down to the water's edge
where the ocean meets the sound.
With her hand in his the Old Man said,
"Just take a look around.

"Not far from here long time ago, a little girl was born;
her name was Virginia Dare.
The first girl born in this part of the world,
'least the first to have blonde hair.

"When told of her birth, all the folks gathered 'round
and sent up a happy cheer.
But soon food ran short, they couldn't go home,
and happiness turned to fear.

"Now, don't know what happened to Virginia Dare;
your guess is as good as mine.
Those people just melted into the swamps,
a place where the sun don't shine.

"But because they came, others would come
and make a life on these shores.
They'd plant trees and crops,
build hardware and grocery stores.

Now, four hundred years later, we've paved miles of roads,
built buildings up to the sky.
But sometimes at night out here by the sea,
I can hear Virginia cry.

"She cries for our land and our people,
land of promise and freedom so dear.
She cries for the woods that are gone now,
for rivers that used to be clear.

"She cries for farms lost in morning mist,
replaced with so many malls.
She cries 'cause we've lost so much of our gift,
we can't hear our heart when it calls."

The Old Man finished speaking by the sea that night;
his words took the little girl back to the wondrous sight
of a brave people who came with only a dream
to be kept alive by the girl in the moonlight beam.

Time Well Wasted

I was on a solitary ramble down one of my favorite dirt roads when I saw Leon Boone fishing in a ditch. It's not unusual to see folks fishing from a bridge across a small swamp run or creek, but Leon was fishing in a ditch: a water channel only about three-to-five-feet wide and four feet deep. It ran from Bogue Swamp and through a culvert under the old dirt road.

I had not seen Leon in quite a while. We had grown up in the same community, and he lived not far from me, though our paths just never seemed to cross. But since we knew each other, I knew he wouldn't think it strange if I stopped to visit with him out in the edge of the swamp.

After I pulled my old pickup truck over to the side of the road, I started walking down to where Leon was perched on a white plastic bucket turned upside down. He was far enough off the road that the shade from the cypress trees gave him some respite from the hot summer sun.

As I walked up, he said, "Hey, William." (People who have known me since childhood still call me William.)

"Hey, Leon. Haven't seen you in a while. Whatcha doin'?"

"Drownin' worms," he replied.

"Not many fish, huh?"

"Nope. But I don't expect to catch any outta this ditch anyhow."

"Whatcha doin' out here with a fishin' pole then?"

"Wastin' time," he said. "There's a cold Mountain Dew in that ice chest over there. Getcha one of 'em and have a seat on that stump."

I did as I was instructed. After I had struggled to get my long, lanky, aging frame situated on the stump, I realized how quiet the swamp was. The moss hanging on the cypress limbs barely moved in the easy breeze. Somewhere in the distance, I could hear birds chirping. The water in the ditch was so slow moving, it didn't make a sound.

The sweet, delicate smell of the bay bushes mingled with the sour smell of swamp water and mud.

As if he'd been reading my mind, Leon said, "Peaceful out here, ain't it?"

"Yep. I kinda like this," I answered.

"Me too. That's the real reason I come out here. Don't nobody hardly ever come by, and I can just forget 'bout all the bad stuff and just think about the good without any interruption."

I sensed that I was one of those interruptions, so I started to get up from the stump. "Well, I just thought I'd stop and see you a minute and ..."

"Aw, sit down, son. You ain't no interruption. Just sit on that stump awhile. Sometimes it's sharing good times that makes 'em good times. Don't say nothin'; just listen to the Lord's creation."

So I tried to "listen to the Lord's creation." What I heard was the silence. In that silence, I began to think like Leon had said he did when he came out to ostensibly fish in the ditch. I began to "think on all the good stuff." I thought about how lucky I was to have had so much good in my life and so little really bad. I thought about all the opportunities I had had to do so many things, meet so many people, see so many places. Then I thought, *How lucky am I to be able to come to a place like this, to renew acquaintance with an old friend, to find a spot more therapeutic than any session held in a psychiatrist's office?*

My reverie was shortened as Leon rose from his seat on the bucket and began to gather himself and his fishing equipment to leave. As he did so, I noted, "You don't even have a worm on that hook! How'd you expect to catch anything?"

Leon laughed as he said, "Oh, I didn't 'spect to catch nothin'. I just needed to give myself an excuse to come out here. Now, if you really want to catch fish, come on down to the lake with me tomorrow, and we'll do some real fishin'. I'll come pick you up at your house 'bout dusk dark or mornin' light, whichever you want."

I thanked him for the offer but said I wasn't much of a fisherman.

"Then you come back down here and fish any time," he said as he laughed and waved goodbye.

A professor told me one time that creativity is being able to express dreams. But first you gotta see the dreams. Leon showed me how to see dreams just by sitting on the side of a ditch with a friend and listening to the Lord's creation. As I got back in my truck, I thought about how my afternoon non-fishing experience had been time well wasted.

Sometimes We See Ourselves Through a Cracked Mirror

A couple of years ago before the pandemic shut down gatherings of more than ten people, I was asked to speak to a group up near Linville, North Carolina. The location was at a country club, and as is usually the case, I got there early enough to set up my table, hoping I might sell a few books while I was there. When I went in the lobby, I saw a little poster somebody had tacked on a bulletin board advertising my appearance at the luncheon. Under my photo was a line that I had heard before but never really thought about. It read that I was an "author, storyteller, and speaker." Usually, such warning to the unsuspecting audience lists only one of those titles.

I had not thought about that designation until recently when I was cleaning out some stuff, including some old booking calendars in my office, and saw that occasion listed. It made me stop and consider which I was: author, storyteller, or speaker. I concluded that the most obvious connotation was that an author writes down his stories and they appear in print, a storyteller tells his stories orally, and a speaker just talks about anything.

After thinking about the definitions of the three designations, I decided I was probably a little of all three. But the one I decided I liked the most was storyteller. I come from a long line of storytellers on both sides of my family. Growing up at my family's general store in a small rural community was like having an incubator for storytelling.

My Grandfather Council used to love to tell stories about the lumber mills and logging operations so prevalent in this area. My uncles Lacy Thompson and Charles Council, both involved in local politics, were always telling stories about past political campaigns in which they had participated or, more often, that they had heard about from somebody else's campaign. My father, Bill Sr., loved to tell stories, and though he often told family stories to my sister and me, his greatest audience was the folks who came into the store or folks who would come out to chat with him while he was pumping oil for their homes or tobacco barns. Toward the end of his life, his short-term memory got smaller and smaller, but his long-term memory gained a renewed clarity. When I would take him from the nursing home over to the old Chadbourn farm where he grew up, stories just flowed about family I had never known, land deals, work at the strawberry crate factory, and Saturday nights at home when he would invite friends over and my grandfather would play the piano and the fiddle—memories and stories that neither time nor sickness could erase.

But by far, the storytellers I most listened to were the folks, Black and White, who came into the store, usually on Saturday afternoon, and told hunting and fishing stories. Most of their stories were farming stories about good crops, bad crops, storms, animals, and of course, people. That was the key element in all the stories: people. Some of the stories were, frankly, gossip, the content changing with each telling. Some of the stories were tall tales, told with exaggerated gestures and imitations of voices. Some were stories of villains and heroes that none of the storytellers had met but who their daddy or grandpa or cousin knew well. Almost all the stories were set in the past, usually the distant past, so that no one could challenge the veracity of the telling.

Truth was not (and is not) a necessary factor in storytelling. In fact, when my sister and I were little, we were not allowed to say anybody was a "liar." If we said somebody was telling an untruth we said he/she was "storying"! And thus my narrative skills were born.

I really miss those days at the store. I miss the camaraderie and the sense of community, usually all wrapped up in a cloud of tobacco smoke, felt hats, flannel shirts, bib overalls, and brogans—all the storytellers seated on upturned soft drink crates. If it sounds like it was all a male-dominated activity, you are mistaken. The greatest venue for storytelling ever invented is a tobacco barn shelter or a packhouse where tobacco is being prepared for sale. I learned a lot about women by listening to ladies in those places. The amount I learned is minute, just enough to know that life has a different perspective for men and women.

When I go to a gathering of people to tell my stories, the stories make a connection. The greatest compliment I can get is, "I knew somebody just like that." And then they proceed to tell me their story. And everybody has a story. Unfortunately, we don't get a chance to hear them like we once did. The old general store gatherings are gone, the Sunday afternoons spent with the cousins at Grandma's are gone, and nobody writes journals anymore.

The new technological age is supposed to make communication between each other easier, but instead, it separates us. Nobody is inspired to tell a story by texting on their cellphone.

Storytelling is an art form as old as civilization. It is the thread that has tied us together as human beings through every disaster—natural and man made. Oral communication predates written. Before there were pictographs and hieroglyphics, people gathered around campfires and probably told stories of hunting woolly mammoths and escaping dinosaurs. Now that I think about it, that tradition is still carried on at some hunting club gatherings!

Whatever the reason, I'm for any occasion that brings us together to talk to each other and remind ourselves who we are and where we came from.

PART 3
MUSIC IS LIFE AND VICE VERSA

Melodies of My World

M usic has been such a big part of my life that I can't decide whether it is the accompaniment or the inspiration. Did I write the music, or did I just sing along? I do know that, without music, it wouldn't be much of a life.

I grew up in a musical family where every gathering included some kind of musical performance by almost every member. My Grandfather Thompson could play just about any instrument "by ear." He played the fiddle for local dances. He would listen to songs on the radio, then immediately play them on the piano or clarinet.

I was going to be a music major in college until my professor and I mutually agreed that, since music theory was a requirement for the degree and much too difficult for me, I should look for another line of work. So I changed my major to journalism, but I still stayed in the music department as part of the touring choir for four years. During that time, I broadened my musical interests to include classical music and opera.

My sister and I grew up singing in the church choirs, of course, but when our Aunt Mary Lee died, she left us a huge pile of sheet music. We went through it all: the syncopated rhythms of ragtime in the 1920s, the big band sounds of the '30s, and especially all the songs of World War II—the songs that could briefly beat out the sound of bombs and the scream of war. They were the songs of a life, a home worth fighting for. Remember "The House I Live In"?

When we went off to college in the '60s, we played and sang folk music for anybody who would listen and especially anybody who would pay us. We were inspired by The Kingston Trio; Peter, Paul and Mary; Joan Baez; and other folk revivalists of the period.

Out of my interest in folk music grew an appreciation for bluegrass. Somewhere along the way, it lost its hillbilly image and evoked the heritage of the mountains and hollers, the mill villages and tobacco fields that are so much a part of who we North Carolinians are. It's back porches and pig pickin's, barbecue and hush puppies, coon hunts on cold nights, and fishing on reed-covered banks.

Even as my musical interests expanded, I was never far from my eastern North Carolinian roots. I still listened to the Grand Ole Opry, the honky-tonk sounds of Earnest Tubb, the silky voice of Patsy Cline, and the plaintive wail of Hank Williams.

At the same time, another Williams boy kept tugging me back home to the beaches, parties, days in the sun. Maurice Williams was his name, and the Zodiacs, along with The Tams and The Embers, made rhythm and blues into a special sound called "beach music." Beach music is more than just music. It's a lifestyle unique to the Carolinas, a lifestyle that cuts across race and social and economic backgrounds. When "My Girl" wafts out over the sand dunes, the soft ocean breeze moves the sea grass, and the moonlight reflects in waves that lap the shore, life has no boundaries, and youth will last forever.

Soon after I graduated from college, I became the director of a boys' choir at what was then Boys Home of North Carolina. I tried to incorporate as many different kinds of music as I thought the boys should appreciate, including some patriotic songs they needed to learn. I think they liked the folk songs and the patriotic songs and even some of the Broadway stuff. Classical? Not so much.

The music of my life is like a multilayered cake. Each layer is separate, unique, and wonderful. Put together, it's a rich, delicious mixture that can't be duplicated or completely consumed.

One of those songs that my sister and I used to sing kinda sums up the role of music in my life. It's the second verse that you hardly ever hear from "With a Song in My Heart" by Richard Rogers. Look it up. It'll make you smile.

Defining Southern Music

Music is always on my mind. That may be because my interest in music is an attempt on my part to escape other things. Then again, music has been such a big part of my life, I can't imagine a time without it. So when I was going to Wilmington the other day, I listened to a public radio station that announced that for the next hour it would be playing Southern music. That really piqued my interest. I definitely would listen to that program.

During the hour, I was glad to hear the subject wasn't only one genre of music. It focused on composers who were Southern or who had a Southern connection. The host of the show had not fallen into the trap of trying to attach one more stereotype to the South. Trying to say there is only one type of music common to the South is like trying to say there is only one kind of music common to anywhere else in the United States. Those of us who are native Southerners are proud of our diversity, not only sociologically but in every other way, including musically.

In all fairness, however, although there is a wide variety of music composed, performed, and listened to in the South, there are some types of music that we all perceive as uniquely Southern.

Jazz often has been called the "only original American music." Certainly, it had its beginnings in the South. Maybe part of it came from the plantations or the folk music of Appalachia or the steamy bars of New Orleans and Memphis. Regardless of its origin, nobody will argue that it contains all the elements we associate with the Southern nature:

rhythm, independence (each instrument in a jazz band usually has a solo in each piece), joy mixed with sadness (the blues), and religion. Jazz is mood music. It may sometimes be romantic, sometimes laid back and mellow, or sometimes energetic and demonstrative. But it is hardly ever background music. (Well, maybe under certain circumstances.)

Then there is beach music. Surely, you say, that is the music of the South. The music we call beach music is relatively unknown outside of the coastal area of the Southeastern United States. The same songs heard elsewhere are called by a different name.

For beach music to be real beach music, there must be other elements involved besides the music itself, elements commonly found in the South: sun, sand, beer, and plenty of time to enjoy it all. All that and a distinctive beat—automatically bringing back memories of our carefree youth when the trip to the beach constituted our major social outing, and finding the right person to dance with was a priority. The essential element of beach music is attitude, a timeless feeling of youth. Sometimes you may start out with it, but you always end up with it.

Then there's country music, the old-time country that often is mournful and sometimes nasal, recounting to music the trials and tribulations faced by most of us each day. Real country music sings about broken dreams, failed love affairs, hard work, no money, too many bills, and an overpowering craving for beer and pickup trucks and trains, among other things.

As I drove along thinking about the radio host's comment about Southern music being only jazz, I remembered a scene from one of my childhood summers on my grandmother's farm in Chadbourn. There was a small unpainted tenant house with no porch, and the front door opened onto two wooden steps. Sitting on the steps was a little boy about twelve years old, and in his lap was a guitar bigger than he was. He was trying valiantly to play it but to no avail.

As dusk began to settle, he put aside his guitar and began singing, "This little light of mine, I'm gonna let it shine," an old gospel song, with only the clapping of his hands for accompaniment.

As that mental tableau faded in the evening sun and my memory, I thought to myself, "That is Southern music!" I didn't mean just gospel music either. I meant singing songs that spring from the heart of the person who sings them just because it feels good.

Road Music for Life's Journey

Some time ago, I was in the western part of the state for a book marketing meeting. I had another meeting for a promotional interview in Monroe. Getting from point A to point B turned out to be kind of a sentimental journey. As is often the case when I am traveling alone, I like to listen to the local radio stations as I pass through the areas of their coverage. So to get a clear signal, I push Scan on my radio dial and listen to whatever comes on. On this particular trip, the first station I picked up was a public radio station near Asheville, I think. The music playing was bluegrass. I like bluegrass. I thought that it was appropriate for the mountains. The program also was an interview with Doyle Lawson, who is a North Carolinian, as are two other members of his band. They played bluegrass gospel, that fast-paced, sometimes raucous, praise and plea for salvation. As I listened to the music, I thought about how representative it was of the people of the mountains, people who were closely tied to the land and who shared a faith that wasn't bound up in ritual and liturgy but was emotional and almost visceral. The lyrics of bluegrass gospel are not likely to have many Latin phrases. The words of the songs are simple, declarative statements and questions; the harmonies are tight, high-pitched melodies that reflect a naturalness unaffected by the rules of music theory.

Many years ago, when my sister and I were in college, we played and sang folk music, usually only for ourselves but, occasionally, for anybody who would pay us to play. That was my introduction to bluegrass. That was the time of America's folk music revival of the 1960s, and our models were The Kingston Trio, Peter, Paul and Mary, and The Brothers Four, among others. Our mentor in the pursuit of our music was Mr. Ray Wyche, our neighbor across the road, who persuaded us to look more for the "real folk music." In the process of following his direction, we listened to a lot of bluegrass. We never *played* bluegrass. We only had a guitar—no banjo, fiddle, or mandolin—and our harmonies were much more subdued. But our research did give us an appreciation of the original music of Appalachia (pronounced *Ap-pa-la-chia*, not *Ap-pa-lay-chia*).

As I headed eastward last week, I was reminded of those days with Linda, of the people who we had met during our folk music period, and what we had learned from them and our experiences. We learned not just an appreciation for the music but also for the people who created the music from their own experiences, who took the sound of the wind in the trees and the roar of the waterfalls, as well as the rhythm of soft waves lapping on a riverbank, and made music.

Of course, I soon ran out of the range of the Asheville station, so I hit Scan again. This time it landed on another public radio station in Davidson. I am familiar with that station since I have traveled many miles through central North Carolina over the years. It plays a wide range of musical styles. I was listening to a jazz program when I got to Monroe for my interview. When I returned to my car and turned the radio back on, classical music was playing. Like many other similar playlists at public radio stations, I sometimes think they try to pick some of the most obscure compositions to play on the air. They don't always announce them, so I never really know what is playing.

Fortunately, the station was featuring a Rachmaninoff program that night, which included a composition I was familiar with because I had heard it in the 1945 movie *Brief Encounter*. Since that film used some other classical pieces, the radio program also featured one of my favorite classic compositions, Bedrich Smetana's *The Moldau*. As I drove through the North Carolina night, the flutes, violins, horns, and the entire symphonic orchestra took me to Europe. The pine trees along Hwy. 74 became fir forests with great stone castles perched on the mountain tops; a scattering of thatched houses lighted by candlelight glowed in the snow-covered lanes that led to the open fields where a thundering herd of horses rushed toward the lichen-covered barns.

Of course, it was just music.

The Davidson National Public Radio (WDAV) station has a strong signal, and it followed me all the way to I-95, where I turned the radio off. I rode in silence as a crazy mixture of bluegrass and classical music flitted in and out of my mind. That's what it has done for my whole life.

You Can Take Refuge in the Music

In my continuing effort to find a respite if not refuge in these troubled times, I decided to try something I've always done when I need something to change my mood. We should always learn from the past, seek out those things that helped us when circumstances seemed to create nothing but obstacles. The thing that helped me most was music. So I tried to remember some of those songs and circumstances.

The very first music I remember was sung in church. We didn't have a nursery for small children then; we sat in the main sanctuary with the adults on Sunday morning (Wednesday nights and Sunday nights too). But the first song I remember singing, we learned in Sunday school: "Jesus Loves Me" by Anna Bartlett Warner.

Jesus loves me, this I know,
for the Bible tells me so.
Little ones to him belong;
they are weak, but he is strong.

My sister Linda and I began taking music lessons when we were very young. Miss Moyers, and later Mrs. Florence Thompson, and especially Mrs. Christine Graham taught us the rudiments of music theory, and Linda became adept at the piano and organ. Our Aunt Mary Lee Thompson was a very gifted pianist, as was our Grandfather Thompson. When Aunt Mary Lee died, she bequeathed all her sheet music to Linda and me. Her music was the accompaniment to World War II and reflected the determination of the Greatest Generation to get through that time. In the stack of sheet music was "Chattanooga Choo Choo" and "Don't Sit Under the Apple Tree," as well as songs of hope like "When the Lights Go on Again" and "The White Cliffs of Dover" by Vera Lynn.

There'll be bluebirds over
the white cliffs of Dover
tomorrow, just you wait and see.
There'll be love and laughter
and peace ever after
tomorrow, when the world is free.

The 1950s was the last age of innocence for most of us. We just enjoyed being young, and the world's troubles didn't seem to be a part of us. We thought that innocence would never end. We bought the 45 rpm recordings of "All I Have to Do Is Dream," "Moon River," and "Oh, Pretty Woman" and shuffled our Weejuns to "My Girl."

But things began to change. The civil rights movement came along, as did the Vietnam War. Those were our college days, and we saw our world reflected through a broken mirror. Linda learned to play guitar, and we got caught up in the resurgence of folk music—the celebration of our heritage, as well as the protest songs, "Blowing in the Wind," "If I Had a Hammer," "The Sounds of Silence," "Where Have All the Flowers Gone?" and the optimistic song that said it all was transitory, "We'll Sing in the Sunshine."

By the '70s, I had gotten married, I had children, had a regular job, and got to sing and emcee at all kinds of events: beauty pageants, festivals, conventions, and lots of other gatherings. I sang the pop songs like "Sweet Caroline," "After the Lovin'," and "An American Trilogy," and we danced under the disco ball to "Dancing Queen," "Stayin' Alive," and "I Will Survive." But the theme song of the time was "My Way."

Over the next couple of decades, pop music seemed to ask more questions than it provided answers: "What's Love Got to Do With It,"

"I Want to Know What Love Is," "What Have You Done for Me Lately." So I returned to my country roots and listened to "God Bless the USA," "Always on My Mind," "I Believe in You," and "Dixieland Delight." I realized that, as Barbara Mandrell sang, "I Was Country When Country Wasn't Cool."

And when the millennium changed, it seemed the music changed. Maybe it was because I was just getting old, but there were few songs that appealed to me.

Some, like "You Raise Me Up," were new, but as I continued to search for respite, I began to play the oldies station on the radio. I looked for songs like "What a Wonderful World," "Let It Be," "Light of a Clear Blue Morning," "He's Got the Whole World in His Hands," and "Bridge Over Troubled Water."

As I wrote this essay, I realized that music had again worked its magic. Just singing those old songs again in my mind made me feel better. We have all come through tough times where we brought the music with us. It doesn't solve the problems, but it makes us feel better.

Worked for me. You try it.

MAKING A JOYFUL NOISE

From the time I was about six years old, I have been singing in some kind of choir. I have directed and/or sung in high school, college, community, oratorio, madrigal, and church choirs. I have never sung in a gospel choir, but I have always wanted to. Nor have I ever sung in a "show choir," a combination of choral music and choreography. All my choral mentors were adamant that we remain absolutely still while singing. This was particularly true of my church choirs, Baptist mostly, who viewed any visual keeping of the rhythm as being close to sin or, at least, encouraging it. I have thoroughly enjoyed the experience. Not only have I been able to be a part of groups that create beautiful music, but I also have met some wonderful and talented people who have become some of my best friends.

As I reach my autumn years, I look back at all those choir experiences and wonder if I might be able to continue to sing in a choir in my next life. What I mean is, if and when I get to heaven, can I become a member of the heavenly angel choir? I assume my experiences here on Earth will serve as an audition. I want to further assume that the criteria for membership in the heavenly choir is pretty much the same as that in any church choir: a love for music and the willingness to sing.

Will I fit in with the celestial singers? To make that determination, I thought I'd take a look at the makeup of a typical volunteer choir much like the one assembled in heaven.

First of all, there will probably be more women than men, and most of the men will claim to be basses. The primary criteria to be in the bass section is "How low can you go?" Being able to match a pitch is a plus, and just singing in the lowest register you can is sufficient as long as you don't sing too loud. There will always be at least one member of this section who will ask what page everybody else is on.

Most of the men in the tenor section have "enthusiastic" voices. They take pride in their ability to reach those high notes, even sometimes going beyond expectations and finding notes up in the musical stratosphere that the composer never dreamed of. Creating a falsetto voice can sometimes be a creative addition. Almost every tenor is a confident soloist and occasionally creates that solo, even if unintended by the composer or director.

In between the tenors and basses will be that netherworld composed of baritones. These are the confident men who smooth out the gaps between the tenors and basses, a rare breed who can come to the rescue of either a tenor or a bass. They have the unique ability to sing the melody line and make it sound like harmony.

In front of the basses are the sopranos, those confident ladies who establish and usually maintain the melody of every song. Once they assure themselves they are singing their designated notes and rhythm correctly, they are capable of moving independently without aide of direction or instruction.

On the other side of the female group are the altos, the ladies who bring a pleasing harmony that rests just a little below the sopranos. Of the five groups, perhaps the altos are the most adept at improvising that harmony, sometimes one completely different from that intended by the composer but nonetheless beautiful.

In the celestial choir, I assume we will be preparing for a cantata. Many of the songs in the special collection prepared for each season of the church year are familiar titles but somehow have been rearranged so the choir will have to learn them like new compositions. The result is a unique performance embracing the old and the new with beautiful music never heard of by either the composer or arranger.

I would be so fortunate to be able to sing in that choir. Volunteer choirs are a part of every community. Those earthly choirs add beauty to the lives of those who listen. I'm sure that applies to the heavenly community as well.

Oh, what a glorious sound that heavenly choir will make! And somehow, I feel sure there will be a full orchestra and hundreds of pianists there to cover up any mistakes. I'll bet not even a heavenly choir sings a song exactly the same way twice.

(Listen to Bill recite this poem, track number 7 on Just Down the Road.*)*

The Benediction

He said, "We come this morning to thank you, Lord,
for the sun and the sky and the earth,
for rain and growin' things,
And for Jesus the Christ Child's birth.

For your love that comes when we need it most,
on the wings of the dove bird's song,
for food and drink and a place to sleep
when the day's been hard and long."

And the preacher said, "Amen!"

Then the old man slowly stood,
for his back was stooped and bent.
But his voice rose like a trumpet's;
his words were heaven-sent!

"Oh, Lord," he said, "I don't ask much,
Just a little food and such.
So when I ask you, Lord, to bless us all,
to cleanse our hearts of fear,
please listen, Lord, just hear my plea
as closing time draws near.

"I've toiled hard in your vineyard, Lord,
worked hard in the boiling sun.
Now I'm old, you see;
my row is almost run.

"But I thank you, Lord, for the life you give me,
for the chance to live in this land.
Now, if you will, I beg you please
bless the rest of 'em, too, if you can."

And the deacons said, "Amen!"

Then the sister stood to raise her voice
in praise of His holy name.
In her robe of white
from the front of the church she came.

A hush fell over the church just then
as the sister began to sing.
And her voice soared high, so high,
made the windows and the rafters ring!

Her voice praised God with a passion rare,
heard only in a heavenly choir.
It was filled with joy and heaped with care
and burned with a fervent fire!

Then her voice got soft, she almost whispered her song,
as tears filled her eyes she sang,
"Oh, Lord, it won't be long."
And the whisper through the rafters rang.

And the choir said, "Amen!"

Then they all stood up in one accord,
swept up in The Spirit's spell.
Their voices rose like an angel choir
as their song began to swell.
And it filled the Earth with Peace and Love.
All is well, all is well.

And all the people said, "Amen" and "Amen!"

THE HARMONICA PLAYERS

Most musical historians say the banjo is the only truly American musical instrument. Certainly, if you count the various adaptations from the original African instrument as the creation of a new instrument, the historians are right. However, I believe the harmonica is an American instrument. It did not originate in America—it came from Europe in the early part of the early nineteenth century—but it became so popular and so much a part of blues and folk music that I think it is uniquely American.

For one thing, a harmonica is relatively cheap compared with pianos and guitars and a whole lot easier to carry around than other wind instruments. It is relatively easy to learn to play. I have one and occasionally play it when no one is around to hear me.

My earliest exposure to the harmonica, like just about everything else in my life, took place right here in Hallsboro when I was a little boy. The occasion was a big deal, considering the time and place. Around 1954, my Uncle Charles Council, manager of Council and Co., the family store, decided to have a promotional event to bring people to the store and keep them there so they would buy items like soft drinks and crackers and Moon Pies and such and maybe, during the process of waiting around, might purchase other items like clothes or hardware.

So he decided to sell raffle tickets for a goat, a female "nanny" goat. I'm not sure why he thought that would be a big draw, but it worked. On a hot July Saturday, he tied a goat to a post in the alley between the store and the old warehouse beside it. Raffle tickets were only a dime apiece, but you had to be present at the drawing when the store closed that night at nine o'clock.

When the store opened that morning, some folks already had gathered to buy their ticket. More people came and more people stayed. Sometime that afternoon, a fellow named Emmett (I never learned his last name.) showed up, and he had a harmonica, which he began to play in the alley.

Emmett accompanied numerous impromptu quartets, duets, and soloists, as well as group singing. Every once in a while, he would play a fast-paced solo. People danced and sang and bought soft drinks and crackers until the store closed and Uncle Charles had me draw the winning ticket. I don't know who won, but I do know there was great moaning and groaning as well as cheering. The winner took the goat home that night, and the promotion was declared a great success. Even as I tell this story, I am reminded that it didn't take much to generate excitement in Hallsboro back then.

As exciting as that event was, I had not thought about it until I went to Charlotte. I took an alternate route south of Monroe to avoid that traffic. Not too far from Monroe, as is my daily custom wherever I am, about midafternoon I stopped to get a Pepsi and a pack o' Nabs at a convenience store. Beside the store was a metal shelter, and under that shelter sat a harmonica player in a ladder-back wooden chair. He was alone. There was no crowd to sing or dance or cheer him on or request a song.

Of course, I noted his presence when I went in the store, though I didn't stop to talk to him. But after I had bought my Pepsi and pack o' Nabs, I couldn't resist going over to talk with him. I pulled up a plastic chair, placed it the proper pandemic-required distance from him, and introduced myself. I told him I liked his harmonica playing. He thanked me for the compliment and asked if I played. I told him I did but not enough to entertain anybody besides myself. He said, "Here, let me hear what you can do with it," as he offered his harmonica to me.

I said, "I appreciate the offer, but I'd rather hear you, and I need to go on and drink my Pepsi and eat my Nabs 'fore I get back on the road."

"Okay," he said. "Watcha want to hear?"

"Whatever you wanta play," I replied.

"I'll play ya one I made up," he said.

He began to blow soft notes that whispered under the metal shed, his hand cupped around the little instrument as he moved the mouth organ back and forth. He repeated the melody a couple of times, then began to play variations on the melody, the volume rising and falling, the tempo still slow and easy, a little bit of "swing" to it. Then that swing became more a part of the sound; it was real blues, the kind that comes from a broken heart and sails up toward the heavens, pleading for grace and forgiveness. Then he just stopped playing. "Played that for my mama's funeral last year. She was ninety years old, and she loved for me to play this here 'monica. Don't play it much. Kinda special song."

I told him I thought it was a beautiful song and I appreciated him playing it for me. I wanted to stay and hear him play some more, but I felt guilty, like an interloper at a private place. So I thanked him again, got in the car, and drove on to Charlotte.

Only a unique American instrument like a harmonica could tie together two disparate images in my mind, a reflection of the diversity of the people who play music at events as disparate as a goat raffle and a mama's requiem.

I Want to Hear It Again

No matter how hard we try, how much attention we pay to details, how much research we do, or how committed we are, we can never create another first time. By definition, a first time can't be repeated. As I get older, I often wish I could re-create some of the most momentous moments of my life. Some I can't repeat because I don't remember them: my first steps, my first words. Some I don't want to repeat; in fact, some I'd just as soon forget.

But as I get older, I naturally reflect on my past. In doing so, I have found that there is one recurring theme for me: music. Almost every aspect of my life has been influenced in some way by music. Some of those times I was a performer, and sometimes I was a listener. But in every case, the first time I had that musical experience, it affected how I proceeded from that time on. Although I can't hear or sing that music again for the first time, I can recall it.

I want to hear again for the first time the sound of a country band with a steel guitar playing in a room so filled with smoke that it looks like the place is on fire. I want to watch again for the first time those nondancers who simply move their feet (and whatever other parts of their bodies still work) to the beat of the music. I want to listen to a song about home and railroads and lost love and pickup trucks and Mama.

I want to hear again for the first time the clear voice of a young soprano learning Puccini's "Un Bel Di, Vedremo" from *Madame Butterfly*. I want to hear that aria ringing down the hall of the college music building to mix with a violin and an oboe and other instruments and other voices to form a beautiful cacophony. I want to the hear the pipe organ in the chapel pushing Bach's *Toccata and Fugue* across the campus on a cold winter's night, accompanying young lovers holding hands as they walk down the brick walkways that weave between the classroom buildings.

I want to hear again for the first time the sea breeze blowing across the sand dunes and lifting the easy rhythm of "My Girl" to the outdoor pavilion where couples dance, their fingers barely touching, their Weejuns sliding across the wooden dance floor. I want to hear the youthful laughter, feel the sense of time and place created there that will be transferred to the next generation and the next, a part of our Southern heritage.

I want to hear again for the first time the sound of a worn-out guitar playing the real blues, the kind that bursts and ripples and weeps and shouts and whispers from the soul of the Black man playing it on the dirt patio of a juke joint where I'm not supposed to be. I want to hear that voice as it sheds a lifetime of struggle and acquiescence at the feet of those like him who have shared that struggle and understand the acquiescence.

I want to hear again, for the first time, the blending of choir voices: a small country-church choir singing those old hymns sung from memory and accompanied by a pianist playing "by ear" on an upright piano with chipped keys; a choir of young boys lifted from home situations where they were sometimes abused and neglected but, through music, lifted above their past; a choir of small children, me among them, each singing his own version of "I Wonder as I Wander" to an audience of family members.

And yes, I want to hear again for the first time the applause of the audience when I sang my first solo as a member of my high school chorus when the football coach who had previously viewed me as most inadequate said, "Damn, boy! You can sing!"

I want to hear again for the first time the comfortable, magical blend of voices and a beat-up old guitar (for which our father had traded a smoked ham) as my sister and I sang the folk songs of the '60s to any group that would pay us, even if the pay was just a meal.

Time doesn't dim the memory of such things. Those sounds are indelibly imprinted in my mind, and I can recall them almost as clearly as if they happened just yesterday. That's a good thing, I guess, since I can't re-create that first time.

PART 4
YOU NEED TO LISTEN TO THE OLD FOLKS ... AND NOW I AM ONE

Eulogy or Elegy?

Sometimes I think trying to write something meaningful causes me to be too picky in searching for just the right word to describe what I'm thinking. And when I find that two words sound a lot alike and have similar meaning, I get so involved in deciding which one to use that what I meant to say becomes secondary. I believe that's called "overthinking." That happened the other day when I was asked to write a eulogy for a friend of mine who recently had died. For whatever reason, I thought, *This is not a eulogy; it's an elegy.* Then I thought, *Well, an elegy is a kind of melancholy poem about someone or something that has passed, and what I'm writing is not a poem.* So it must not have been an elegy for my friend because it was not a poem.

A eulogy is prose written as a more celebratory mourning of someone or something that has passed. That got me to thinking about how much our lives have changed and that we are sad it has changed but glad it was a part of us. (See what I mean about overthinking?)

I began to think about this change in our perception of who we are as Southerners and North Carolinians. What has not changed that we can still celebrate? What has changed that we now mourn? I realized that I have probably written more about the small towns of North Carolina than any other topic: the small town I grew up in and that surrounded me all through my youth, and the small towns I traveled to, celebrated with, and loved have changed, but in my mind's eye, they will always be the same. Even as we experience the growth of the cities, and the distance between towns gets shorter, the essence of North Carolina is still there along the two-lane roads.

I like to eat breakfast in the little cafes where everybody knows everybody, and all the problems of the world get solved every morning before eight o'clock.

I like to go to the community parks where children play baseball and soccer, parents sell hot dogs and popcorn to raise money, and grandparents in folding chairs watch the babies in folding strollers.

I like to read the local papers that carry the school menus along with the results of the last town council meeting.

I like to look at old courthouses and imagine the lives changed by the activities that went on in those buildings.

I like to walk through old tobacco barns and smell that unique aroma of curing tobacco that still lingers there.

I like to attend community festivals that celebrate every living thing, as well as every real and imaginary historical event that may or may not have happened there.

I like to watch parades where local bands march and play and beauty queens and politicians perch on the backs of convertibles.

I like to hear church bells ring on Sunday morning and homegrown choirs singing the hymns in the same church they sang in when they were children.

I like to go into the local clothing store where the clerks know you by name, remember what size you wear, and don't care if you want to buy a suit that went out of style ten years ago.

I like knowing that a letter sent to me without a zip code or even a complete address will still reach my mailbox.

I like to walk the streets where front porches are still for sitting, where air-conditioning is reserved for the hottest evenings, and where the smell of hamburgers and charcoal mixes with the perfume of a newly mowed lawn in the summer.

I guess only time will tell if I should change all that into a poem or just make it a eulogy.

A Place Too Small

Some folks think living in a small town is a good way to shut themselves off from the "real world." But it's not. A small town is a part of the real world. But there are some people who want to live apart from people, to remove themselves from the possibility of sharing life with anybody, people for whom other people are unnecessary.

Of course, there is something reclusive in the personality of each one of us, something that makes us want to "get away from it all," at least for a while.

If we have one of those modern jobs with a lot of technological gadgetry and a lot of public contact, we probably feel the urge to retreat from the pressure more than folks in less chaotic vocations. Sometimes we withdraw by going to some other place like the beach or the mountains. It may be just a short time to be absent from our usual surroundings. Maybe we do come back.

But what about that person who is always "away from it all?" Would we want to be like that?

I thought I might have a hint until I met Homer Cashwell. Homer is alone. Really alone. He lives in the middle, or near the middle, of the Great Dismal Swamp on the North Carolina-Virginia border. He is there because he wants to be, and he says he is not lonely.

On a drive home from Norfolk one summer, I stopped at a little store for my usual afternoon snack: a Pepsi and a pack of Nabs. Homer was there picking up some groceries. I had heard about Homer from the store owner on a previous trip, so I was glad to finally see him in person. Being not the least bit shy, I asked Homer about his life in the swamp and the inherent loneliness. He replied with a surprising openness for a man who shuns company. He said, "God made everything around me: every stump, every snake, every vine and sinkhole. And he made me. So I'm part of it all. How can I be lonesome?"

At first it sounded pretty good to me. As I talked to Homer at the little grocery store on the bank of the canal near South Mills, he seemed to be content with his life and, for a person who shunned company, was quite open and talkative. He told me he had no electric bill because he had no electricity. He had no car payment because he had no car. His only transportation was a little flat-bottomed boat. His sole income was a government disability check.

As he squatted on the store's little porch, he said, "I ain't got an enemy in the world 'cause I don't owe nobody. I ain't got what you'd call friends neither 'cause they'd always be a-wantin' somethin', so I don't cultivate 'em. I'm my own man."

That was about the extent of our conversation. I watched him as he bought some items and loaded them in his little boat tied to the bank of the canal and wondered what would make a man choose such a solitary life.

"He's sort of a legend around here," the storekeeper said. "Some say he come back shell shocked after the Vietnam War and couldn't stand being around people and noise, so he just took hisself off to the swamp."

I watched Homer paddle his boat down the canal back toward his little house in the swamp. I knew that when he got to that house, there would be no one there to meet him. There would be no one there to share his evening meal. He would sleep alone. The next day and the day after, his conversations with nature would be one-sided monologues.

The world would continue to pass on by Homer Cashwell, the world of noise and pollution, of conflict and strife, of wars and famine and hate. But the world of love and humanity also would pass him by, a world that cares about disaster victims in a country far away as well as the ones next door, a world where neighbors bring food to a mourning family and pray for people they don't even know.

Homer has chosen to shut out the world—the good and the bad. By doing so, not only did the world lose a valuable human being, but Homer lost the warmth of the human touch—something more valuable than solitude no matter how hectic our lives may be.

I like sharing my life with other people, especially those in a small town.

"Land Is the Only Thing That Lasts"

once proposed that a major criterion for determining whether a person was a real North Carolinian was his degree of fondness for boiled peanuts. I figured that if you had gone so far as to have served boiled peanuts as an entrée, you may qualify as a native North Carolinian. I came to that opinion based on my own fondness for the legume and the shared opinion of just about everybody I knew. The opinion was that boiled peanuts are one of the premier products of the Carolina soil, a food to be savored and appreciated in every household and with the same reverence as collards and grits.

Alas, I found my opinion was not universally shared. In fact, many North Carolinians north and west of Raleigh not only failed to share my love for boiled peanuts but looked with disdain on them. Some even ventured to say that they were not "fit to eat."

So it was with some interest that I stopped to visit with a roadside produce vendor back a few days ago. There was a big hand-painted sign out on the highway that proclaimed, FRESH BOILED PEANUTS. Boiled peanuts in season—hot, juicy legumes recently plucked from the soil and still soaking in the briny water—are uniquely satisfying to a country boy who grew up in the swamps and sandy fields of southeastern North Carolina. Such produce transcends the bounds of mortal nourishment and becomes the nectar of the gods. Such is the force that drew me from the traffic of modern life to the seductive (metal) tent of the peanut vendor.

There is something about outdoor markets, something that is at once temporary but something that also transcends time. It's easy to envision the ancient open-air marketplaces where the products being sold were produced by the salespeople. Such is this produce stand, all sides open to the breeze that blows across the produce, wafting the collective smell of the earth, the same now as it was thousands of years ago.

My wife, epicurean that she is, loves to stop at these places to peruse the more mundane products of the soil: peaches, apples, melons, delicious butter beans and peas, onions so pungent they tickle your nostrils, and purple and white turnips with a little bit of the dirt still attached. She can take those items and magically turn them into culinary masterpieces.

As she considers the possible purchase of those succulent items to grace our table, I linger by the boiled peanuts. I savor the smell of the steam rising from the large steel pots that have been placed over butane burners. The smell of the boiling peanuts triggers a memory of the days of my youth when I toiled in the peanut fields, digging the bushes from the ground, then picking the peanuts off and placing them in wooden baskets as I sat on the tailgate of a pickup truck laden with the harvest.

My reverie is broken by the voice of the vendor, "You want some of them raw ones or the boiled ones, buddy?"

I am torn between buying the finished product bagged and ready to be eaten or prolonging the sweet agony by buying the raw peanuts still cool and waiting for my own personal treatment that will imbue the pure, untainted gem of the earth with the unmatched flavor that only comes with the knowledge of a process handed down by generations of boiled peanut connoisseurs.

Life is too short to ponder such decisions for very long. With the wisdom of Solomon, I buy some of both: some to eat as I go down the road and some to prepare when I get home.

The enjoyment and appreciation of boiled peanuts is a legacy I want to leave to my children and their children yet to come. My brother-in-law and my son-in-law, both products of that culinary chasm of earth north of Maryland, cannot abide boiled peanuts. Therefore, it is left to me to ensure their children's awareness of their culinary heritage. Boiling peanuts is a part of their heritage, a tie to the land from which we all spring and to which we will all return. As Gerald O'Hara once said to Scarlett, "Why, land is the only thing in the world worth livin' for, worth fightin' for, worth dyin' for. Because it's the only thing that lasts." Just like boiled peanuts.

Thoughts on the Road Less Traveled

On my way home from Elizabeth City some time ago, I decided to take the road less traveled. Highway 17 is the most direct route back to southeastern North Carolina, but I wanted to go "the old way" on the roads I had traveled all those years since I began crisscrossing the state on a regular basis more than fifty years ago. I wanted to revisit those little towns like Pactolus and Bear Grass and Greenevers and all those other little wide places in the road that happen to have a sign designating their existence.

I didn't need a GPS to find my way. (In my car, GPS means Gone Past the Sign.) I could follow those old two-lane roads from memories of so many days and nights coming and going to speak to all kinds of groups and celebrating so many festivals held in the small towns and cities.

It was midmorning when I left Elizabeth City, so the sun was behind me as I headed in a generally south-southwesterly direction. The sun didn't cast too many shadows on that flat land. I could go for miles, and the tallest things I would see were a few pine trees in the distance and acres and acres of corn and soybean fields. Small, neat little houses sat in the middle of the fields, and behind the houses were old tobacco barns tilting to the side, their rusted tin roofs resting on rotten wooden sides held up by vines.

In the midsummers so many years ago, those fields would have been filled with tobacco plants, their big green leaves lapped over each other row after row, soaking up the hot sun. And somewhere in that field, bent under the big leaves, were men and boys "cropping" the leaves from the stalks. Their shirts would be soaked with sweat as they rose with their arms filled with the leaves, then placed them in the "drags" or trailers that would take the crop from the field to the curing barn. I have worked in fields like that.

Of course, folks today don't see those fields as I do. Today tobacco is a bad thing and, certainly, its use is not good for you. But I couldn't help but reflect on what tobacco had meant to so many families like mine. I guess it depends on your perspective as to what tobacco means to you.

If, when you say "tobacco," you mean that noxious vegetation which, in its processed form, creates a smoke that permeates the lungs of young and old alike, eating away the tissue of that organ of life and emitting a smoke that causes a stench in the clothes we wear, the furniture on which we rest, and the very breath we breathe; or if you mean that agricultural endeavor whose harvest has caused young men to toil in the heat of the day until they collapse from exhaustion; or if you mean that dried weed whose dust clogs the nostrils and fills the lungs until they are as black as a sinner's heart; then I am against it.

But if by "tobacco" you mean that product of the Carolina soil that has been the source of livelihood for thousands of families for generations, that provided the funds to send the sons and daughters of poor tenant farmers to college, that built churches where the loving spirit of the Creator is made known to all who enter its doors, that kept many an able-bodied man off the welfare rolls and filled the coffers of every clothier, grocer, and merchant in every small town across this state; if you mean that commodity from which the sale thereof created the taxes that paved the roads that now traverse the length and breadth of this great state, that built the schools that educated and continue to educate the leaders of our communities; if you mean that golden leaf whose heady aroma emitted from the curing barn wafts across the summer night, weaving its spell like the perfume of a beautiful woman; if you mean that product that has given solace and comfort to those who have come to the end of the day in which they have struggled mightily to make a living from the land or who finally have found a respite from the heat and monotony of the mill; if you mean that smoke created in the bowl of a pipe as men sit together in commonality and devise solutions to those social ills that beset us; if you mean that cigar proffered as congratulations at the birth of a child or reward for achievement; if you mean that crop whose history is irretrievably tied to the existence and development of this state, the South, and this country, then, my friend, I am for it.

I thought about that driving back from Elizabeth City. I guess it all depends on how you look at it.

In Search of Comfort Food

There is probably nothing more central to Southern culture than food. It is an essential part of everything we do. We prepare special foods for every occasion. We take it to the neighbors when they're sick or when somebody dies. We celebrate weddings and birthdays and any other occasion that we can generate that might be a venue for serving food.

Many folks, including my wife, center their lives around the planting, cultivation, harvesting, and preparation of food. Conversations at almost any gathering eventually come around to how our gardens are growing, the latest recipes, the menu at the new restaurant, and what was on a particular television cooking show.

There is a whole genre of cuisine called "Southern cooking" that is revered by some and reviled by others who consider it detrimental to our health. There are those, like me, who are aware of the hazards of so much of what is determined to be Southern cooking, with its abundance of butter and preparation of things in boiling grease, but love to eat it anyway.

So when I heard some folks say they needed some "comfort food," I wondered how they managed to narrow that category down from the vast array of comestibles available to us. Was some food comfortable and some uncomfortable? I first tried to determine if it was the food that caused the comfort or if it was merely the circumstances around the consumption of a particular food that created the comfort.

After considerable deliberation and a lot of actual tasting, I determined that comfort food is mostly in the mind of the one doing the tasting. Once again, I strengthened my belief that, "Everything in the world is personal."

The first food that came to my mind, the food whose consumption caused me to immediately feel good about my immediate circumstances, was boiled peanuts. I have written and talked at length about my fondness for this legume. My association with this product of the soil harks back to my early childhood when I would help my grandmother pick the goobers off the vines, prepare to wash them, and place them in boiling water with enough salt to float a battleship. My family, every available generation, would sit on the porch or in the yard as we cracked the shells and eagerly ate the peanuts hot from the shells in which they were boiled. Conversation and laughter would mix with the breeze that blew across the tobacco fields and under the pecan trees.

But probably the happiest venue for eating boiled peanuts was in the tobacco warehouse as my sister and I would sit on piles of neatly stacked tobacco just prior to the auction of the now-disdained leaf. The tobacco sale represented the culmination of a lot of hot, tedious labor that resulted in money to pay for school clothes, mortgages, and higher education for a lot of people in southeastern North Carolina. You have to admit, that's a very comforting feeling.

The other food of my childhood that still tastes as good as the memories that preserve it is cold watermelon in the summertime. I try to reproduce the splendor of its consumption as often as possible. You pick the watermelon from the field in the late afternoon, place it somewhere where it will cool overnight (like a well or creek), then the next afternoon you cut it lengthways into long slices and eat without the assistance of utensils.

In determining what constitutes comfort food, I have to mention a personal favorite that confirms my proposition that comfort food for one is not necessarily comfort food for another.

I love liver and onions on a bed of hot rice. I have had people tell me I have a warped pallet. When I was growing up, my mother would sometimes fix this dish for our evening meal. I guess one of reasons I still enjoy it is the memory of the aroma that always accompanied that particular supper as Mama prepared it and I played outside with my sister and the kids in the neighborhood until the night would creep up on us and Mama would call us to come in. Liver and onions smell like home.

Then I thought of what is sometimes referred to as "soul food": collards, butter beans, fried anything—particularly chicken and pork chops—steak with rice and gravy, baked sweet potatoes, corn on the cob, field peas mixed with white rice (called Hoppin' John), little Irish potatoes, and fried okra or squash. Usually, this food was served for Sunday dinner or any special time when the extended family was at the house.

Yeah, comfort food is a personal thing.

The Fairy Tale Fiddler

Once upon a time, a fiddler came to town. Actually, he was a violinist who came to Whiteville with an electric violin and an amplifier so it was possible for his music to be heard outdoors. He didn't come to play a concert in an auditorium but stood in the middle of the Food Lion parking lot on the north side of town.

Street musicians are not a common sight in Whiteville now. Not too long ago, there would be a plethora of performers on street corners and in tobacco warehouses during the height of the tobacco sales season. Singers, instrumentalists, even dancers displayed their talents. It was just a part of the excitement of that bygone culture.

And as in every fairy tale, the people came from all around. Maybe they didn't come just to hear him play; after all, they were at the grocery store. When I arrived at the scene and heard the music, I asked a friend of mine where the music was. "It's over there," she said as she pointed toward the front of the parking area.

"It almost makes me cry. It's beautiful."

So I immediately went to the site of the performance and saw a young man playing the violin. Beside him stood a young woman holding a small baby. I listened to the music and watched the young man. There were several people around him wrapped not only in the music but in the moment of sharing the music in an unexpected place.

I listened for a while before I continued into the store to make my purchases lest I forget what my errand was. On the way in, I noticed two lovely young ladies whom I knew were knowledgeable musicians. "Whattaya think?" I asked.

"I love it. We just bought some wine and were thinking we might open it and sit on that bench and enjoy them," one of the women said. They laughed.

I rushed through my errand, came back out, and immediately decided I needed to get to know this artist. I didn't interview him; I just talked with him. I found out he had come to Whiteville from Italy by way of Charlotte on the way to Myrtle Beach. He was a professional musician who had fallen on hard times since the pandemic had closed down so many venues that could accommodate the orchestra with which he played, as well as many other venues. He had a hand-lettered sign with his name "Ali" and his telephone number on it, citing his availability to play for weddings, funerals, and any occasion that would benefit from his music. His violin looked unusual, just a simple board with strings on it, and when I asked about it, he said he used it for "marketing purposes," playing for audiences wherever he could find them and hoping someone would hire him. He lived in Charlotte, but he had friends in Myrtle Beach, and he traveled back and forth and would stop at other shopping centers and "audition."

I asked how old the baby was, and he said, "Three months and the joy of my life." I asked his wife if it was a boy or girl, and the man said, "She doesn't speak English. My baby is a boy."

"I bet he changed your life," I said.

"Yes," he answered. "My wife, my baby, and my music are my life. I play for them and for me."

I didn't talk to him long because people were asking him to play. So I stepped away and listened to the music. I also listened to the audience, people on the way to buy produce and meats and ice cream. "I love it." "He's not really playing it." "I haven't heard music like that in a long time." To a little girl, "Wouldn't you like to play like that one day?" "Hey, you good, bro!" "My mama would love this." "He's 'bow-syncing' [lip-syncing for violin]."

To me, the music was beautiful. Even the people who doubted the authenticity of the performance liked the music. Art is in the eye of the beholder. As a Southern gentleman, I think that music is like Southern women: all are beautiful, some more so than others.

And all the while, the music lifted from the concrete parking lot and over the parked cars until it was absorbed by the passing traffic. That was the magic of the Fairy Tale Fiddler. In the middle of a mundane world, in a parking lot in a small town in eastern North Carolina, we mortals were listening to the same music heard by other people around the world. For a little while, music of the Vienna woods and the palaces of Europe changed our surrounding to green meadows or a royal court. Music can do that, you know.

Country Roads

Over the years, I have developed a fondness for country roads. Unfortunately, the old dirt roads are disappearing, and the opportunities to drive on the paved back roads that wind through the woods and fields are becoming less and less available. But that doesn't keep me from thinking about them, writing about them from time to time, or asking people where I can find such old avenues of travel.

Weeds grow quickly on old farm roads. Nothing impedes their growth—no modern vehicle traffic, no plethora of pedestrians stamp it down. Its most frequent traffic is old dogs, some in pursuit of romance and some in packs, scavenging for a meal.

Most people don't care where those roads lead because people with a destination have no reason to follow a road that goes to no particular place. But if we look carefully, we can see ourselves along these roads. Our ancestors came down these roads, not only those pioneers from centuries ago but recent kin—grandparents and great-grandparents, the aunts and uncles we used to see at family reunions. We listened to their stories and saw in our minds what took place along those roads.

These were wagon roads long before the automobile and pickup truck were invented. The wagons came to little houses built by the hands of people who lived in them. No contractor was needed to build their homes. The wagons brought their spartan furniture—often handmade— shuck-bottomed chairs and three-legged stools, butter churns, beds with rope springs, and tables made of three wide boards.

The most lasting thing the roads transported was people. The roads ran a long way from town. It may not seem like a great distance today, but if you had to walk or ride a wagon to get there, it could be a "fer piece."

If we take the time and make the effort to traverse these roads today, we see only the remnants of a life that was once bursting at the seams with agriculture. It was a life literally built from the ground up. The soil grew not only crops but also a spirit of independence that was taken for granted until it was gone.

For most of North Carolina, particularly here in the eastern part of the state, tobacco was the heart of the economy. It could provide a decent income for families who didn't have a lot of land. For a long time, the labor-intensive operation didn't lack for workers. Families were big, and there were plenty of people available who needed the work, including the neighbors who swapped labor, each family helping the other as needed.

Now those roads that saw the wagons and trucks loaded with neatly bundled piles of tobacco have no traffic. Much of society has said that the very item that sustained life for those farm families caused the death of others. So the roads are empty.

Those roads that provided access to a new life for those long-ago families are the same roads that so many of today's farm families travel as they leave their farms. Modern agriculture has no place for the small family farm as it used to be. The transition to mass pork and poultry operations has peaked, and the other alternatives are few. Although they may be riding in their cars and trucks instead of walking or riding in a wagon, it's still a long way to town.

The floods and hurricanes of the past few years have washed away much of the soil that once nourished those fields of tobacco. Those roads have been flooded by storm water; some of the old bridges that once covered the little creeks and streams have been washed away, some replaced, and some creating a terminus since nobody used the roads anyway.

After a recent heavy storm, an old man stood on the porch of the country store and told the traveler about the effect of the floods on his fields. He pointed out the devastation of his crops, the loss of his livestock, and the destruction of property. Then he summed up the plight of the farmer, a situation not understood by people who had not traveled those country roads. "Heck, it don't matter. I couldn't make a livin' on it no more anyhow. Then again, I ain't never tried growing rice."

That's the kind of perseverance that has kept the Carolina farmer going down those country roads all these years.

I'm reminded of a prayer I saw on a plaque at St. Giles Cathedral in Edinburgh, Scotland. It was written by Robert Lewis Stevenson, but it could have been whispered by the farmers across the fields and woods of eastern North Carolina:

Give us grace and strength to forebear and persevere.
Give us courage and gaiety, and the quiet mind.
Spare to us our friends, soften to us our enemies.

LIVING WITH THE SEASONS IN THE SOUTH

I was born here in the South and am proud and glad of it. But one of the characteristics of living here is that the summers are hot—not just warm but oppressively hot. I also grew up before the advent of air conditioning and, therefore, had to find ways to keep from being overcome by the heat. Sometimes that effort took some creativity. Considering the recent news about climate change causing more heat, I thought I would share some of my recommendations of ways to beat the heat. I must confess that some (well, most) came from neighbors and friends who, like me, have lived in the small-town South during those hot summers. Indeed, there are several options, some of which you may enjoy.

1. **Sweat.** That is the first option. It does not require much effort. Indeed, all you have to do is exist. Having said that, there are some Southern ladies who do not sweat. They merely perspire. In so doing, they take on a glow that enhances the natural beauty of those ladies who were born here and whose natural gentility is enhanced by the moisture created by the summer sun. I have been told by some dermatologists that perspiration moisturizes the skin and creates a softness that cannot be matched by the finest creams or emollients.

   However, if those ladies adhere to the practice of "laying out" or basking in unprotected sunbathing, they face the chance of sunburn. Some Southern ladies protect themselves from sunburn by wearing large hats when outdoors at social events. But I have noticed that those same ladies will go to the beach clothed in just enough fabric to keep from being arrested. There must be some feminine logic there, but I long ago ceased trying to figure it out.

2. **Find a cool place to rest.** I personally like to find a large crepe myrtle or other arboreal bower that an occasional breeze wafts under. Sitting on a shaded porch not only presents a respite from the sun but also allows for contemplation or conversation. There was a time when neighbors joined each other on porches to spend time discussing matters of the day—weather ("Ain't it hot!") or crops ("This heat is killing my tomatoes.").

3. **Grab a cold drink.** Whether on the porch or under a shady tree, a cool libation—particularly sweet iced tea—is the perfect accompaniment. Southern hospitality often may include a snack to go with the tea, such as boiled peanuts or ice-cold watermelon, or, for those with a less sophisticated pallet, pork rinds.

4. **Get in your car.** Do not turn on the air conditioning. It will spoil you. Roll down all the windows. Place one arm (the left one if you are driving) outside the window. Drive the speed limit while your hand moves up and down with the wind created by the moving vehicle. Wear a short-sleeved shirt or blouse so the wind can blow up your sleeve.

    If you are fortunate enough to have a convertible, put the top down. If, by chance, it should begin to rain, leave the top down.

5. **Go where there is a lot of water.** This may include a lake, pond, creek, river, or swimming pool. Some even have found solace in a wide ditch. Whatever body of water you may choose, by all means,

check for snakes and alligators before entering—even some swimming pools. Remember, they were there first.

A good friend of mine, Reverend Leon Henry, is an evangelist. He said he is more likely to have people come forward and accept Christ as their savior in the summer. He said that baptism in the river in the winter causes some people to put off their salvation until the weather is warmer. However, I believe that hot weather might make them more aware of the consequences of their decision.

6. **Pray for rain.** Ask for one of those "scattered showers," not a thunderstorm or certainly not a hurricane. A small shower, as it is coming down, will cool the air and is almost always followed by a cool breeze. Do not be afraid to go out in the rain. Walk in it, dance in it, roll around on the wet grass, step in the mud holes. It is probably best to remain clothed while out in the rain unless you live far away from your neighbors or passing traffic. You may find similar surcease from the heat by turning on the lawn sprinkler.

Remember the old instruction for happiness? "Dance like nobody's watching." This applies to dancing in the rain. Debbie Reynolds and Gene Kelly enjoyed it in the movie. And by the way, Brandi Carlile wrote a song in which the lyrics said, "You can dance in a hurricane, but only if you're standing in the eye." Remember that during the next hurricane.

7. **If all else fails, turn on the air conditioner.**

Then sometime toward the end of the year, it all changes; we have to say goodbye to small-town summers.

Every year the passing of the seasons brings something when it begins and takes something away when it ends. Between that seasonal alpha and omega are sights and sounds and smells that remain with us through to the next season, an expectation that life continues bringing with it the good and the bad. The changing of the seasons is kind of a promise, kind of an optimistic one that the past will pass, and the future will arrive, and what we want to change will change, and what we want to forget will not appear.

Leaving should be accompanied by goodbye. So I thought I'd say goodbye to my small-town summer and hope it will return and be much like it was.

Goodbye to morning mist rising off the field pulled by the rays of sun streaking between the clouds.

Goodbye to watery diamonds hanging on the flowers, sparkling on the green leaves, waiting to disappear like magic in the morning light.

Goodbye to the green carpet that covered my lawn that is now covered in tan insulation, awaiting its resurrection come spring.

Goodbye to the crepe myrtle bower that provided respite as I toiled in the summer sun. It's a place where a breeze always blew the heat and humidity away.

Goodbye to the long dusk where the sun takes its time going behind the pine trees, that time when the dogs lie napping on the porch and the birds are nesting in the magnolia trees and the azalea bushes.

Goodbye to the smell of newly mown grass and hamburgers cooking on the grill.

Goodbye to silence at midnight when the constant traffic in front of my house is almost nonexistent, and the faraway sound of the big trucks is just an assurance that the old, man-made world still exists.

Goodbye, summer. See you next year.

And the future should be greeted with hello.

Hello, autumn.

Hello to new gold and brown and tenacious green.

Hello to corn harvests, big machines and dust, and husks flying across shorn fields, and corn pouring copiously into big trucks.

Hello to the smell of burning leaves, to the memories of families gathered to clean the fallen arboreal detritus.

Hello to crisp, cool mornings that cry out for a sweater that will be shed by noon.

Hello to evening fires in fireplaces that have lain dormant only to rise from their lethargy to warm the body and stir the memories of those gathered around.

Hello to quiet walks across wide fields in the company of friends and bird dogs ostensibly in search of quail but all content to soak in the silence with a reverence for the nature with which God has blessed us.

Hello to quiet beaches, to solitary but not lonely walks, with the cry of the seagulls blending with the soft sound of the waves lapping on the shore and the sight of sea grass bending slightly in the breeze.

Hello to football games on Friday nights and to the camaraderie of young and old as they gather to cheer on the local high school teams.

Hello to the orange school buses taking children to school in the morning and returning them home in the afternoon.

And yes, hello to the first frost sparkling in the morning, a beautiful, fresh white carpet stealthily announcing the coming of winter.

So the seasons change, marking the passage of time, illuminating our lives with nature's wonders, and giving us hope that those things that cause us pain will pass and those things that bring us pleasure will return.

The Change of Autumn Horizons

Every fall for nearly twenty-five years, I began the school year as either a student or a teacher. Now I am neither. But the cooler air, the changing of the colors in the trees, and all the news about the challenges facing schools due to the pandemic make me think of a different time. My memories of friends, teachers, ball games, and even some academic recollections are mostly fond. But nostalgia is a great editor of our memories. It casts a shadow over those things we would rather forget, those things we wouldn't want to do again, even knowing now the things we didn't know then. And that's the way I want to leave it.

Life is too short to think of all the "might have beens" or the "if onlys." Looking back doesn't hold the excitement of the first time things happen. We already know the result of the past. What's the fun in that? It was the uncertainty of the future that made life so interesting.

We older folks are often asked, "If you could go back and do your life over, what would you change?" I have to say, "Not much." Frank Sinatra sang of regrets that were too few to mention. I had rather remember each fall when I'd see the friends I knew from the first through the twelfth grade. In our little rural school, there wasn't much turnover in the student body. We had all been born there, and we wouldn't leave until graduation. If you see the same people almost every day for all those years, you form bonds that never break, even over long distances and no contact.

Then when I went off to college; it was a new adventure with new people—some from places I had only read about in *National Geographic* and some from other exotic places like Raleigh and Charlotte and Stedman and Kinston.

My life went from being carefully supervised to—well, it was still carefully supervised on the Baptist campus of Campbell College in little Buies Creek in the early '60s. It wasn't until I went to Chapel Hill as a graduate student that my life was restricted only by my own decisions of conscience and the laws of municipal, state, and federal government. Oh, what freedom, relative as it was!

One of my professors at Campbell was a wonderful lady who had been there almost since the school was founded. She taught English grammar, and we began each class with a prayer. She was as concerned about our moral development as she was about our academic progress. On one occasion when one of her students was unable to perform in class as well as was expected due his weekend revels, she chastised him by declaring there in class, "I know why you are so unprepared. You were over at Chapel Hill this weekend, carousing with those infidels and smoking cigarettes!"

When I later joined those "infidels" in Chapel Hill, I experienced another adventure, another expansion of horizons that I had never envisioned back in Hallsboro. Certainly, my studies expanded my intellect, but that was a time when life as we knew it, particularly in the South, was changing. The state legislature and the college disagreed on who could speak on the campus. The speaker ban limited who could speak on campus, and there were student protests. Imagine the reaction of a former student on the circumscribed Buies Creek campus! My horizon expanded, no, *exploded*. All of that was a part of my education as much as the classroom.

This coronavirus pandemic has changed our world. School isn't the same as it used to be and probably never will be again. I think we may all be the lesser for it.

Wish It Hadn't Changed

It is probably not unusual for folks like me to complain about change. We have been doing things the same way for so long that doing it any other way is a personal challenge to our sense of right and wrong. However, some things that change are not necessarily right or wrong, but they are different, and our preferences don't fit the change.

I guess my objection to change is most evident when it comes to food. I grew up in the rural South and had the privilege and honor of being supplied with nourishment by some of the best cooks in the world. I guess that's why biscuits that come in a frozen pasteboard can fail in comparison to my mama's and grandmamas' biscuits. But probably the worst comparison is the butter they made and the butter we now buy at the grocery store. Homemade butter has been determined to be unhealthy. The pasteurization process makes the old procedure using raw milk unlawful. There was a time when we drank milk just like it came from the cow. Even the milk we bought was delivered to our doorstep every morning by the man who operated the dairy just down the road. The neck of the glass bottle it was delivered in held the most delicious cream you ever tasted. And if you combined those biscuits with that butter and a tall glass of cold milk, you tasted a little bit of heaven.

There are many things now that are instant. I guess it's natural for us humans to be attracted to anything that is easier to do. Food preparation is a task no matter how you look at it, and if the cook can find a quick and easy way to put dinner on the table, I don't blame them. But that doesn't mean I don't miss real grits and real pancakes and bacon that sizzles in the frying pan. In all honesty, I have to say that some cooks come near to masking the instant preparation of baking goods. Cakes, pies, and muffins made from a mix are sometimes almost undetectable from scratch made.

Probably one of my biggest disappointments was my first drink of instant cold-brew decaffeinated sugar-free iced tea. We really ought to call that something else; it is not real iced tea. Real iced tea is brewed in a pot on the stove using tea leaves and hot water. There is enough sugar placed in that tea to make the liquid just short of syrup. Then it is poured over large chunks of ice into a tea glass, which is anything from fine crystal to a Ball canning jar, and served at every meal. Some people add freshly squeezed lemon juice just to give it a little bite.

According to my doctor, drinking a lot of sweet tea is bad for me. I have been consuming gallons of the fine libation for over three-quarters of a century. When he told me overindulging in sweet tea could shorten my life span, I told him I could spare a few years and kept on drinking.

One other change I really miss is going to the barber shop and not smelling pipe or cigar smoke. When I was growing up, Mr. Ed Baldwin had a barber shop almost next door to my family's store in Hallsboro. Mama said I had to get a haircut every two weeks whether I needed it or not. I don't know how much it cost, because I never paid Mr. Ed directly. He "made a note of it" and sometimes would get enough Red Man chewing tobacco at the store to take care of my account.

While I was getting my hair cut, there was usually somebody in there smoking a pipe or cigar. There was always some kind of interesting conversation going on: hunting and fishing stories, stories of busted moonshine stills, logging accidents, mule sales and purchases, and the inevitable discussion of loose women. To a small boy, the smoke and the conversation meant I was a part of man's world. No girls allowed. Now, as I reflect on those innocent days, I know that the smoke was bad for me and most of the discussions were lies. But I'd love to go back and do it all again.

A Look at Life's Verities

As I have now reached that age that some refer to as "elderly," I look back on what I learned from my elders: my parents, grandparents, and some of my uncles and aunts. (Some of my uncles and aunts were my age.) In retrospect, I have found that most of the verities of life I have learned came from their instruction or example. I recently realized that almost all of those people have passed on, and I felt like I should write down some of these truths so that those who follow me can benefit from them.

I guess the first thing I should mention is that we should have respect for our elders. I know sometimes young folks think old people are out of touch with modern culture. In some cases, that may be true, but it doesn't mean that all the experience of our lives isn't still applicable in this changing world.

Take manners, for instance. I have written many times about the lack of civility in today's world, how people consider—or don't consider—the feelings of the people with whom they interact. Manners are just one element of civility. A man should stand up when a lady enters the room. (I don't want to hear a lot of discussion on what constitutes a lady. A woman is a lady until she proves differently.) We should open doors for the people behind us when entering a building. We should say "Yes, ma'am" and "Yes, sir," "No, ma'am" and "No, sir." I know of some younger ladies who consider "ma'am" an insult; it's not. It is a sign of respect.

There are a lot of other acts of respect and manners, but that's a good start.

When you drive down the road and meet a funeral procession, pull over. It's a sign of respect not only for the deceased but also a way to let the family and friends know that we share in the sadness of the passing of another human being.

Write thank-you notes for any gift, even Christmas presents. If somebody does something nice for you, let them know with a personal, handwritten note acknowledging their act. Remember, if you are writing to young people, they may not be able to read the note if it is written in cursive.

Regarding note writing, I think all of us should write more notes or, at least, send cards to those we love, letting them know we love them. We certainly should tell them as often as possible, but sometimes a note or card will serve as a reminder until we get to see 'em and hug 'em.

I thought of one thing that doesn't have anything to do with manners but is an essential element of respect for fellow humans. Teach your children—boys and girls—about gun safety. Here in the South, guns are a part of just about every household. We should make sure that young folks know the dangers of handling a gun in an improper manner. The hardest way for them to learn would be pulling over for the funeral procession of a friend or relative who was killed by a gun.

One of the most important things I learned from my elders was to do what's right regardless of how many are doing wrong. I remember Mama saying, "Just because Jerry will jump off the Cape Fear River bridge doesn't mean you should." Sometimes truth comes with the simplest expression.

I'm pretty sure that the best instruction I ever got was from my mother when I would leave the house to go somewhere with my friends. She always said, "Y'all be sweet now, you hear." That about covers all interaction with people.

The Stuff of Life

I spend a lot of time in my little office in my house. Technically, it's not an office, at least, not a business office, since very little business takes place there. A painter friend of mine said I should call it a studio because I create art (books, stories, etc.) there. However, I am reminded that "art is in the eye of the beholder," and some folks would say what I create is not art. Some would say it is not even creative.

My office is a repository of my life. Like a lot of folks, I collect stuff. My stuff is eclectic to say the least. I'm not a collector of any specific item like bottle caps or stamps or anything in particular. In fact, I don't know that I actually sought out most of the stuff I have collected. It has been given to me by people I have met, some close family and friends, as well as some acquaintances and some people I didn't know.

I won't enumerate every single item in the little room, but I can say that there is very little of tangible value there. Nothing in the room could be used as collateral for a loan. But to me, the contents of the room are invaluable.

A couple of years ago, my only grandson, Drew, came for a visit. During the days he was here, we had occasion to spend some time talking in that room. We talked about a lot of things, some things grandfathers want to pass on to their grandsons: family stories, old photos, a fountain pen. We also talked about his place in the family. He is the only grandson, but his surname is not Thompson. He is my daughter's son, and my son has all daughters. We talked about what that means. During our conversation,

I gave him some personal items: an old wristwatch of mine, a couple of books, some of those old photographs. I told him that when I died, he would get much of what was in that room, and I began to tell him what each item meant.

Teenage boys have a short attention span. I had told Drew about the old roping saddle I had in the corner that had been given to me by my uncle, about the old rolltop desk that my mother gave me, about my grandmother's old quilt and rocking chair, about the sketch of The Old Place where my mother was born, about my father's portrait on the wall. He asked me about all the diplomas and plaques and citations I had hanging on the wall and the old guitar in the corner. I was telling him about the old wooden desk chair that my Granddaddy Council had used when the young man interrupted, "Granddaddy, what are you going to do with all these old books?"

He had been looking around the room while I was talking. He had looked at the shelves full of books that filled up the walls on every side. I didn't have an immediate answer to his question. I had never thought about the absence of those books. They had accumulated over years: some of my old college textbooks (literature, no algebra), books by authors I knew with personal messages scribbled on the inside, and classics that dealt with the South like *To Kill a Mockingbird*, *Gone With the Wind*, *Let Us Now Praise Famous Men*, *You Can't Eat Magnolias*, and *The Old Man and the Boy*, among others.

There are books by contemporary Southern writers like Pat Conroy, Flannery O'Connor, Eudora Welty, Charles Kuralt, John Grisham, and, of course, Lewis Grizzard and Roy Blount Jr., just to name a few. And the ones I have written are up there too. There are a lot of history books and biographies.

I don't know how many books are in that room. There is another roomful downstairs and a bunch in the storage room next to the office.

They are not well organized. There's no system of order, not even alphabetical. But I know where to find each particular title if I want it.

I had not thought of those books collectively until Drew asked me about them. The collection, I wouldn't call it a library, has been a part of my life for a long time, in several different houses, through several different jobs. The number has increased, and I have loaned some to folks. Some were even returned.

What I have read in those books has become a part of me, formed my way of thinking about people, politics, sports, literature, religion—life. I can't picture my life without them. So my answer to Drew was, "I don't know." I think my daughter, who reads as much as I do, will have some interest in them. Maybe Drew and his cousins will read them. I've read some of them more than once and used some for reference.

I still don't know what I'm going to do with all those books. I know I'm going to keep them as long as I live, although they are "stuff," like the other items in the room. But they are the stuff of life.

It Ain't About the Money

As I have gotten older, my attitude toward holidays has changed a little. When I was very young, I looked forward to those celebrations that included gifts. Christmas was the biggie in that regard, followed by Easter, which meant new clothes. Of course, as I got older, the true meaning of those religious celebrations became more important to me.

Then there is Valentine's Day. It is named after a saint and is a religious holiday in some denominations, but most folks don't see it as a religious celebration at all. Most of us see February 14 as a day to buy flowers or some other gift to show how much we love that special person in our lives.

When I was in grade school, we exchanged cards with our classmates— all of 'em. The special ones got little peppermint hearts.

So, in keeping with my revised attitude toward holidays, I rethought my definition of a Valentine's Day gift and how it relates to love. I came up with a few conclusions based on my own often-woeful experience, as well as what some other people have experienced in the love department.

What says more about love than a gift on Valentine's Day?

Love is sitting up all night in a hospital waiting room by yourself. I know that in this modern age, the option of the father in the delivery room could change the birthing experience, but there are other occasions that could apply to those waiting room experiences as well.

Love is watching her sleep. She doesn't have her makeup on or her hair brushed, and those wrinkles are a little more obvious. But somehow, she still looks like the girl you married so many years ago.

Love is the feeling you get watching your son get his first haircut or watching your daughter's first dance recital.

Love is bringing her flowers you picked yourself when it's not a special occasion. (A bouquet of wildflowers counts extra.) Special occasions like Valentine's Day take all the spontaneity out of gift giving. Her reaction to the unexpected is a cherished picture. It also makes her wonder what you're up to.

Love is when you enjoy her beating you at Monopoly or *Jeopardy!*. When that happens, just hint that you let her win, even if she beat you fair and square. Then run like crazy.

Love is when she fixes your favorite meal, even when she is as tired as you are.

Love is the smell of baby powder. First of all, baby powder just smells good, but sometimes the greatest value is to replace the smell of dirty diapers. Real love is when you change the diapers.

Love is when she just walks by your chair and gently touches the top of your head. That little action indicates a familiarity that only the two of you share. And, as the song by Steve Allen says, "This could be the start of something big."

Love is wearing that pink shirt she bought you. You haven't worn a pink shirt since the days when Elvis was your hero, but now you are her hero.

Love is watching a Lifetime channel movie together. It's real love if you can watch two in a row.

Love is holding hands in the car while driving to the grocery store.

Love is making up your own poem for a Valentine card instead of buying one already written.

Love doesn't mean never having to say you're sorry. Love is saying you're sorry and meaning it.

Love is forgetting why you had an argument. (As you get older, that gets easier.)

Love can be confusing. It can make you so sad you want to cry and so happy you want to fly—at the same time.

Love is one of those things you don't have to catch or mount on the wall to remember how great it is.

Love is like money: no matter how much you have, you always want more.

Love is letting her drive without telling her how, as you sit beside her, gripping the door handle.

In looking back at these observations, I noticed that money is not a major factor in any of them. So my conclusions are as follows:

1. Love ain't about the money.
2. Valentine's Day is once a year. Love doesn't have a calendar or an age limit.

Dream a Little Dream

Every year or so, more often now, my high school class holds a reunion. Like so many small towns across the South, our school was proportionally small—only sixty in the class, only seven hundred in grades one through twelve. As I thought about that the other day, I wondered how many of us reached our dreams. Did we set goals, or did we just dream dreams? I thought about the relevance of looking back. Is it worthwhile to look at our lives in retrospect and measure our accomplishments against our goals and dreams? I think it is. A quote from Shakespeare's *The Tempest* came immediately to mind: "We are such stuff as dreams are made on; and our little life is rounded with a sleep." If that is, indeed, the case, then it is certainly worth looking back because the past tells us who we became.

Of course, I can't speak for my classmates. I don't know their dreams or what their aspirations were when we were finishing that part of our lives and reaching for the door to the future. We were leaving the confines of home, the security of family on whom we relied for their wisdom—wisdom that was based on their experiences.

I believe we all had dreams: small dreams and big dreams with intermediate goals. We may not consciously have planned our future, and some of us didn't even know what the next step was. For me, I knew I was going to college. I didn't know why or what I was going to major in. I tried music for a while, but after three semesters of music theory, we—my advisor and I—mutually decided I needed to get in a different area. So I chose English. It's worked out pretty well.

I know we all had dreams of some kind. We had the wistful-hope dreams, short-term dreams like getting a date with a particular girl. The pop music group The Mamas and the Papas borrowed a song from Doris Day, "California Dreaming," that echoed that dream.

My dreams in that regard were short dreams that stretched out for years. When you are a certified nerd like I was in high school, those dreams took on a permanence. I didn't have a real date until I got to college, and some of those were nightmares.

Sometimes those short-term dreams became true. I was talking to a lady the other day who told me her dream in high school was to get married and have a family. Once that dream became a reality, she extended her goal and decided to go back to school and pursue a degree. I had a college professor who told me once that the key to success was setting achievable goals but always moving the goal line. That's good advice no matter your goal.

When we take that retrospective look at our dreams, some of us will be disappointed. Things didn't turn out like we planned. That's not always bad. Sometimes our dreams were ill-planned and were not to be. Sometimes God has a plan He didn't tell us about.

In my retrospective view, my life has surpassed my dreams. I never would have thought an old country boy from Hallsboro would have the experiences I have had. Most of my dreams have come true, and a lot of what I have experienced has been way beyond anything I ever dreamed of. All without much help from me. In fact, I probably made enough bad choices to cancel out a lot of dreams, but God persevered when I screwed up. He took what talent I had in music and writing and created a life with few regrets.

In the Bible, Acts 2:17 reads, "And it shall come to pass in the last days, saith God, I will pour out of my Spirit upon all flesh: and your sons and your daughters shall prophesy, and your young men shall see visions, and your old men shall dream dreams," (King James Version). I'm not to the dreams part yet, but I'm getting there.

As an old boy raised in a small town in the South, I am not averse to quoting scripture and Shakespeare at the same time. In *Twelfth Night*, Sebastian says, "If it be thus to dream, still let me sleep." The other poetic line that comes to mind was written by Robert Browning. He said, "Come, grow old with me. The best is yet to be."

All that applies to me: old age and sleep—perchance to dream. I don't want to stop dreaming.

But sometimes dreams and reality conflict.

A fellow asked me the other day, "What would you do if you had all the money in the world?" I told him I'd pay my bills as far as it'd go. Of course, that was a purely hypothetical question since the actual acquisition of such an amount of money is impossible. But it did make me think for the hundredth time how much money is enough and whether by "enough" we mean enough to live on or enough to be happy.

Thousands of young people will be graduating from high school in the next few months. They are in the early, tentative stage of making decisions about their future, particularly what occupation they will pursue. It ain't easy; neither is making the decision nor living with it.

Many years ago, I was the director of the Atlantic Center for the Arts in New Smyrna Beach, Florida. It was a nonprofit agency, funded primarily by the Rockefeller Foundation and the National Endowment for the Arts, to bring selected students to the center from colleges and universities throughout the South for a period of time to study with and become acquainted with well-known literary, visual, and performing artists. It was a sort of reverse artist-in-residence program.

One of the big fringe benefits of my association with the project was the opportunity to get to know these artists (and the students) and to sit in on the lectures and workshops and, most importantly, those informal conversations on the deck that spread over the marsh that housed the campus. On one occasion, we were fortunate to have Miss Eudora Welty spend six weeks on the campus. She is probably (still) regarded as one of the most outstanding authors of the modern era, especially for those readers who, like me, have a particular interest in the literature of the Southern United States.

Miss Welty was the quintessential Southern lady. She was always very polite and wanted to encourage young students to pursue a literary career, if that is what they really wanted. However, she cautioned them to realistically pursue their dreams. One statement she made that has stuck in my mind as I have pursued my own writing career was, "Always remember that art is a great way of life if you have another way to make a living." I have heard other people make that same statement about other occupations, especially farming, and its truth remains the same.

Miss Welty's caution was not meant to dissuade those budding artists from following their dreams but to make them aware of what they would have to sacrifice to reach those dreams. Almost every artist that visited the center while I was there came to encourage and enhance the talents of the students, to make them better writers, painters, sculptors, photographers, dancers, singers, etc. But I never heard any one of them say that money was a primary objective.

Beverly Sills had just retired from the New York City Opera when she came to spend a few weeks with us in Florida. Like Miss Welty, Miss Sills was supportive and encouraging as she gave those students the benefit of her experience in the mutual career they had chosen to follow. She, too, told them of the sacrifices they would have to make to reach their goals. She told them of her own struggles despite the tremendous talent she brought to the opera stage. But she always emphasized, "It was worth it, and I'd do it all again!" Her other quote that I will always remember is: "You don't have to be a star to be successful. You don't have to be satisfied with your achievements. But you do have to believe that you are doing something worthwhile and you're giving it everything you've got because that's what you want to do."

Those of us of a certain age are prone to fits of retrospection, to look back and wonder, "What if …?" and sometimes to ask, "Is that all there is?" Not many of us have reached any level of fame or fortune even if we sought it. For most of us, we sacrificed at least part of the dream because we had to make hard choices: to put food on the table, to provide a place to live, to take care of the family. But we never stopped dreaming the dream, not always about art, but still a dream.

There will always be dreams and dreamers. Some dreams will come true. But above all, I hope we will keep the perspective: our dreams should make us and the people we love happy, regardless of how much money we have.

Thoughts When Leaving a Small Town

Over the past fifty years or so, I've spent a lot of time traveling throughout the South at night alone in an automobile, usually on return trips from speaking engagements. If I had nothing scheduled in the area for the next morning (and because I'm too cheap to pay for a hotel room), I'd make my way back home.

Most of those trips were to small towns. Many were to speak to civic clubs that used to exist in every crossroad community. I would ponder on the comments I heard from the club members and reflect on the conversation with folks at the service stations where I would stop. The conversations, wide and varied, stuck in my mind.

A result of those lonely excursions is a weird (for lack of a better word) reflection on the state of the world, my neighbors, and the earth in general. Many years ago, I would try to remember those thoughts the next day but to no avail. Later, I got a little tape recorder to take with me so I could record my musings. Recently, I found that old tape recorder. The batteries were dead, and the tiny tape was so scratchy I could hardly understand what I had said even after I had put new batteries in. But I listened to it all as best I could and realized some of what I had said was pertinent only at the time I said it. In other cases, I found that I had made some observations that might hold true even today. Admittedly, some—maybe most—of them are trivial, but I wrote them down this time.

1. Nobody will ever put a sign out that says NICE DOG.
2. I believe that the average woman talks 50 percent more than the average man listens. I also believe that no woman thinks she is average.
3. There's no such thing as a "simple little job around the house." Every job becomes complex because I don't have the right tools or someone comes along who will tell me a better way to get the job done.
4. Eventually, everything we do or eat will kill us.
5. I believe smoking is the leading cause of statistics. Never in the history of mankind has anything been studied by so many with so little objectivity.
6. You should never eat prunes when you are hungry.
7. The greatest investment in the world today is computer paper. (I recorded this thought at a time before everything was recorded on CDs, USB, or any of the other modern computer devices that have replaced paper.)
8. I believe it's logical to assume that a fat person uses more soap than a thin person. In all honesty, I have no empirical evidence to substantiate this statement, and the possibility of gathering any is highly unlikely, given the nature of the study.
9. There is no such thing as half a hole.
10. You can't convince a stoplight that you are in a hurry.
11. Nobody really cares about apathy.
12. The man who invented the eraser had a lot of insight into human nature. However, his genius would have been wasted had someone not invented the graphite pencil.
13. Most people use credit cards because they don't have enough money in the bank to cover the transaction.
14. The United States Constitution has to be the greatest document ever written. How else could this country have survived all

the politicians who have tried to manipulate it? (Remember, I recorded this several years ago.)

15. In this imperfect world, there is not a solution to every problem, but there is a problem for every solution.

16. The government can never be run like a business because the boss (or bosses) can be fired by the employees.

17. I am convinced that the best definition of infinity is one lawyer waiting for another. (This was based on my experience at that time of dealing with lawyers every day. Probably hasn't changed.)

18. If other people's problems ceased to exist, most of us wouldn't have anything to talk about.

I'm glad I don't take any more of those long night trips by myself.

If George Washington Came Back to My Town

Almost two and a half centuries ago, the United States came to be, and now, every year, this country celebrates Independence Day. It took a while for it to get its footing, to create a constitution and unify (more or less) the thirteen states. It took a little while longer before the new citizens felt like one country. Some felt so more than others, and by the middle of the next century, those who didn't feel a part of the country seceded and created their own confederacy of states. Four years of bloody division ended, and the union was united again.

I have often wondered what George Washington would have thought of the Civil War or, as some folks call it, the War Between the States or the War of Northern Aggression. But even more speculative would be his opinion of his country today. Would he recognize the modern model of a democratic republic that has evolved since he and those other patriots pledged their lives, fortunes, and sacred honor to create this country? What would he see?

He would see riots in the streets. This country was born in protest—a protest against, among other things, taxation without representation. Those folks who threw the tea into Boston Harbor were protesting the unfair taxation on tea. But they didn't burn the ship or take any of the tea home with them. That would have made them thieves instead of patriotic protestors.

He would hear fiery, vitriolic exchanges on the floor of Congress. Kind of like the exchanges between Aaron Burr and Alexander Hamilton, but the modern exchange wouldn't include a duel.

He would see only about 1 percent of the population involved in agriculture, but the 1 percent is sufficient.

He would see people walking and sitting while looking at a small instrument and ignoring the people and the world around them while relying on somebody else to provide them information about the world. Kinda like the earlier scribblers and the first newspapers that espoused the opinion of the publisher. If a citizen didn't like that newspaper, he'd find another publication that mimicked his opinions.

But if George Washington came to North Carolina, to my little town, on a Fourth of July weekend, he would see some other things too.

He would find my young friend, Bryson Dockery, studying the Constitution, an article and amendment at a time, learning what it meant and what it means now. Then he would see that young man get on one of those social devices and tell other people what he has learned.

He would see three children behind a produce stand in front of their house selling vegetables to people lined up to buy their products not only because they are good but because the children are selling them, bagging them, and making change.

He would see people gathered in the backyards, beaches, rivers, and lakes to cook and eat together. There would be Black and White families together, eating hot dogs and hamburgers and somebody boiling peanuts and somebody cutting cold watermelon because we live in the South.

And he would see American flags lining Main Street and flying from porches and flagpoles. It wouldn't be the flag he knew. It would be the flag of fifty United States. The states would still be disagreeing, sometimes vehemently, but like family, they still are one.

John Adams, George Washington's contemporary and the third President of the United States, said at the signing of the Declaration of

Independence, "It will be celebrated by succeeding Generations as the great anniversary Festival. It ought to be solemnized with Pomp and Parade ... Games, Sports, Guns, Bells, Bonfires, Illuminations ...."

If Mr. Adams and Mr. Washington had come to My South, to North Carolina, to Hallsboro, they would have heard church choirs and congregations asking God to bless America, practicing that freedom of worship for which they fought. They would have heard and seen fireworks over stadiums and lakes. I wish they could have seen the spectacular fireworks display put on by my neighbors just down the road. They would have sensed the significance of the display as it lit up the sky over the big cornfield around my house. They would have seen a tribute to the land, to the people who farm it and the people who live in it. If George Washington had come back to my town, after adjusting to modernity, I think he would be mostly pleased with what he had helped to create.

Some Things Always Look Southern—Like White Bucks

I've got two pairs of white buck shoes in my closet. One pair is about worn out, so I bought the second pair to wear so I wouldn't look as used up as that old buckskin. That's what happens sometimes, you know. Our countenance reflects the condition of our shoes and vice versa. That's where the old expression "down at the heels" comes from. I still wear the old shoes when I want to be comfortable and don't have to worry about looking proper.

White buckskin shoes are proper footwear when you want to feel stylish during the summer, particularly down here in the South. They go with just about everything, especially a seersucker suit of any color. I've got blue, gray, and brown seersucker suits I love to wear. I saw a light red (pink) seersucker suit one time that I thought about buying but decided it would make me look too much like an ice cream salesman.

White bucks are stylish for summer wear because you just don't wear white shoes before Easter or after Labor Day. Some other traditional rules that have developed over the years are the following: wear white socks with white bucks, don't wear them with black slacks, and keep them only moderately clean so they don't look like they are brand new. White bucks and khakis are always correct. (Just an aside. Down here in the South, khakis are proper attire for just about every occasion short of a formal wedding or a funeral.)

White bucks are dress shoes, but unlike other dress shoes, you can't polish them. You just take a stiff brush or a big rubber eraser to get the scuff marks off. With other dress shoes, you can polish them to such a high sheen you can almost see your reflection. My old bucks don't shine, but they reflect a lot.

When I look at those old shoes, I remember my youthful days, wearing some like them to lawn parties (called garden parties if there was a lot of shrubbery), where there were beautiful girls in bright sundresses that showed off their dutifully acquired tans. There was usually a band set up on the patio, with beach music wafting through the night air, mixed with the smell of perfume and newly mown grass. Paper lantern lights suspended in the trees cast a soft glow like stardust over us while the white bucks shuffled and spun and flirted with the dyed-to-match pumps of the girl whose fingertips just touched mine as we danced the night away.

Those old shoes also transported me to hundreds of festivals celebrating everything imaginable in small towns and big cities throughout the South, events that brought together the diversity of the communities while extolling the unique elements that justified the celebrations. My white bucks seemed to fit right in with the boots and flip-flops, high heels and sandals. There was always a luncheon or a pig pickin' where everybody wore little name tags and greeted each other with hugs. Sometimes we'd sit at picnic tables or on bales of straw or find any flat surface where we could place our paper plates and plastic cups while we stood and talked and laughed. And under a pecan tree, a bluegrass band would play, their high-pitched harmonies and fast-paced instruments setting the tone of excitement and optimism.

I've worn my white bucks to countless wedding ceremonies and receptions. I've worn them to outdoor nuptials where threatening clouds in the distance were dismissed as being too ephemeral to cast a cloud on the occasion. But I have also run for shelter as those clouds dampened the proceeding, everybody waiting too late to escape the rain. My white bucks got wet and muddy as I dashed across a drenched lawn or raced to the car through a dirt parking lot. But those shoes clean up pretty well, surviving with a touch of class.

I had a friend who lived at Wrightsville Beach back during the early '80s. His house had a big wraparound porch always full of flowers and ferns. White wicker furniture spread around the porch, the blue-and-white print cushions lending light and color to the comfortable resting spot. Everything was ordered but relaxed. He had a few friends over after the garden party at Airlie Gardens during the Azalea Festival, and I noticed that all the men, including me, wore white bucks. The shoes just sorta came together with the porch ... and the gin and tonics and the little finger sandwiches ... and the boiled peanuts.

Sometimes White Bucks Aren't Appropriate

When we get right down to the reality of style, white bucks are simply shoes. They are attire for the feet, support for the body, and accompaniment to the clothes we wear. But it seems to me that my white bucks have a unique quality. They create memories.

But sometimes, the traditional white bucks aren't appropriate. One late afternoon I was at Lake Waccamaw and decided to drive down to the dam at the mouth of the Waccamaw River. I had no particular reason to go there, but I hadn't been in a while, so I went. When I left the Boys and Girls Homes farm, the sun was shining and the white fluffy clouds were drifting slowly across the sky. There were still a few hours of sunshine left before the night would black out everything except for a shadowy view of the lake and its environs.

However, the scene changed quickly as I drove along the canal road. A few raindrops hit the windshield of my car, and then a torrent of rain fell just as I pulled into the parking area at the dam. There were a few people rushing off the bridge that goes over the mouth of the river. They quickly left in their cars, and I was alone except for a small car parked right in front of the sign indicating the Waccamaw Water Walk.

As often is the case, the rain was just a short shower. However, as it ended, the sun was still hidden by the dark clouds, and the whole scene was quiet. As I sat in my car, I thought this would be a good time to check out the water trail. I had not been down that path and figured the rain had cooled the temperature enough to make a short walk comfortable.

There was enough breeze to blow the yellow flies away, and the snakes would be in the water since it had rained.

I headed down the path that started in front of the dam. I could hear the water rushing through the dam, and I stopped to watch it pour through. It didn't make much noise, just enough to break the silence.

The water path was clearly visible—not marked as such, but you could walk where there was no grass. I could easily avoid the dark tree roots that emerged from the wet sand as I walked along the river's edge. Right at my feet, I could see a fallen tree that lay submerged at the bottom of the shallow river. I wondered how long it had been there. Had it been cut by man or blown down by a storm? Since there was nobody to question my speculation, I figured it was a victim of one of the many hurricanes we get around here. Then, on second look, there were no limbs on the trunk of the tree. Someone must have cut them off. Why would they leave the trunk in the bottom of the river? Probably no way to get it out. Just something to think about on a quiet, wet walk by the river.

I turned to go on farther down the riverbank. It was still clear—no mud holes, no limbs to block the way. I saw a flash of white to my left as a heron rose gracefully from the other side of the river and landed a few yards ahead of me on the upturned stump of a fallen tree. I stood quietly watching the beautiful bird, its long neck arched into an S shape. In just a few seconds, the bird rose again and disappeared into the swamp farther down the riverbank. I had been standing under the limb of a sweet gum tree, and the drops of water from the leaves of the tree were falling on my head. I took that as a sign to move on.

I had gone only a short way when I spotted a big turtle on the end of a log that was projected out of the river. At the other end of the log was a small alligator. Neither of them moved—nor did I until I sat down on a wet, fallen log. I watched them for a while, wondering about the outcome of that encounter. After several minutes, neither of them made a move. It could have been an extension of *The Peaceable Kingdom* painting; two natural adversaries (if a turtle can be an adversary) resting on the same log. The fact that one could consume the other doesn't fit that picture though.

I rose to head back to the car and put my foot down into a mud hole. That was the first time I had remembered I was wearing white shoes. Buckskin shoes are appropriate footwear with anything except funeral attire in the summer. Or if you plan to go for a walk in the swamp. Fortunately, it was a sandy mudhole, and the water was clear. Still, the term "dirty bucks" had taken on a new meaning.

As I walked back to the car, I met a lady coming toward me who also could have been inappropriately dressed almost anywhere else. She had on a pair of denim bib overalls with the legs stuffed into rubber boots. She also wore a very frilly red silk blouse, long dangling earrings, and a white baseball cap.

I greeted her and asked where she was from. She said she was from Wilmington and had come to the river mouth to take photographs. I wished her well and continued back to my car. I wondered if she had worn that outfit in her car all the way from Wilmington, or had she changed into it after she got to the lake? Anyway, who am I to question a person's appropriate attire? I was wearing white bucks in the swamp.

Is There Still a South?

Several times in my column, I have mentioned that I am a Southerner and proud of it. A lady in the drugstore read one of those articles and later asked me to tell her where the South was. I told her that most often when people refer to the South, they mean that geographical region of the continental United States that rests generally south and southwest of the Mason-Dixon Line, located somewhere north of Maryland. But a lot of folks think the South is comprised of those states that formed the old Confederacy.

The lady who asked me that question was, as we say in the South, "not from around here" and wanted me to know that she now considered herself a Southerner since she had lived here more than half of her life. I told her I was glad she had joined us. She smiled, thanked me, told me she liked my columns, and gave me a hug. That gesture, particularly in the middle of a pandemic, told me that the lady had really made the transition. Most of us are huggers, and the pandemic has strained our self-control almost to its limit.

On my way home, as often happens when I make unscripted replies to complex questions, I began to rethink my description of the South. Over the years, I have been honored to participate in many discussions, symposiums, panels, seminars, and other gatherings of folks who sought and continue to seek a more definitive answer to "what is the South."

Almost every time, the general consensus is that the South is not a geographic designation. It is a continuing, evolving concept, more a state of mind than a collection of cultural perceptions and assumptions. This is probably true now more than ever as mobility and communication have expanded until we have almost become amorphic, even homogenous, so similar that it is difficult to see the differences that distinguish us from anybody else in the world.

Often, we have relied on stereotypes to find out differences. Sometimes these stereotypes come from movies or television. How many people think all Southerners are rural and that rural connotes uneducated, crude, violent, and ugly? The term "redneck" is used to define that perception. Let me hasten to say that rednecks do exist in varying degrees of rudeness. However, just as there are rednecks, there also are many educated, mannerly, nice-looking (even beautiful) people who live in the South, and they exist in all geographic areas and cross all racial and social barriers.

Despite the assimilation of all other cultures, here are a few things I still perceive as Southern.

1. **The Southern accent, the true version, not the one imitated, is indicative of our background.** Without going into all the linguistic history that created that distinctive speaking pattern and pronunciation, I would say the Southern accent is a pleasure to listen to. When I hear that intonation, I am reminded of the folks working in tobacco and cotton fields, in the swamps and forests, the guys talking about racing horses and automobiles, the preacher seeking to save souls, and the folks in the mills working in the heat and lint so that the next generation can go to college. I like to hear that. That's *my* South.

2. **Everybody talks about the heat.** That is a part of what makes us different. My daughter was in Arizona once and told me it was hotter when she got home than it was in the Arizona desert. I know; it's the humidity, and nobody else wants it. So the heat and

humidity will continue to be unique characteristics of the South whether we want them to be or not.

3. **Famous chefs have taken the Southern food, our mothers' and grandmothers' cooking, to international status.** But regardless of the effort, unless you grew up with that almost intuitive knowledge of Southern cuisine, you cannot match that taste. It has to come from a small kitchen, maybe even cooked on a wood stove. It has to been seasoned with family tradition and served with a humbleness that belies the exalted origin and commands an elegance even when it is served on a tattered tablecloth. And no matter how hard folks try to make 'em good, or how much they charge for 'em, boiled peanuts cooked in a pot anywhere else will never taste like those cooked in an iron pot over an open fire in our backyards. And the meat-and-three cafés with the country/soul food will never prosper elsewhere unless a Southerner takes it there.

4. **Then there's dirt.** I put this right after the food because some folks think we eat dirt in the South. We may eat dirt if we slide into home plate head first or get thrown from a bucking horse or some other mishap. But we don't eat dirt on purpose. We love the land. We love the sight and smell of plowed fields. We love the sandy beaches, the shaded riverbanks, the pastures and hay fields, the woods, and even the dirt roads. We like the earth. It's a part of us.

There are other elements of the South that continue to make us different, but I don't have space to go into all of them. It is safe to say that a reverence for family (especially Mama), an appreciation for beautiful flowers, regular church attendance, dogs, and a love of pork barbecue cooked on an open fire are a part of us that can't be transported elsewhere with the same value.

I have often said, "Everything is personal." The South is personal to me. It is my home, warts and all.

But sometimes people can't see past the warts. It makes me wonder if we are really making any progress.

Is Change Always Progress?

One of the most unfortunate consequences of the coronavirus pandemic was the closing of libraries and bookstores. The unavailability of new books or library books has been a source of consternation and frustration for folks like me who like to read. (As a writer with a new book out, the closing of bookstores has been an additional frustration.) Since new books are unavailable, I have resorted to rereading books in my home library, some I haven't read in many years. During my retrospective reading, I came across a book I had purchased in 1972 in the Atlanta airport. I remember being initially drawn to the book because of its title, *You Can't Eat Magnolias*. I am always interested in reading anything about the South, and this turned out to be a collection of essays by prominent and well-known writers, as well as sociologists and some other folks who were observers of the uniqueness of this region.

It was published by an organization called the L.Q.C. Lamar Society that was founded in North Carolina with its headquarters in Durham. Frankly, I don't know if it still exists or if it was just a short-lived organization. The organization was named after a nineteenth-century Mississippi political leader who was a model of progressivism after the Civil War. Essentially, the book was a proponent of "the New South" that felt whatever problems we had at the time could be solved not by addressing things like racism, poverty, and lack of education directly but by placing emphasis on industrial and commercial growth. Its members believed those obvious negatives existed but felt their new approach based on industrialization and the resulting improved economy would solve those age-old problems.

Without going into a normal review of the book, I will just say that most of what they proposed worked. North Carolina, in particular, became a leader in education. The economy, based on tobacco, furniture, and textiles, was a boon to every layer of Tar Heel society. But as I further reviewed what cultural progress we had made in the last half century, I looked through some other commentaries I have in my library that have been written since 1972. Folks like Bill Farris, Bill Friday, Bill Powell, John Shelton Reed, and several other people who wrote about creating a more progressive South and North Carolina, in particular. And, not to put me in the same category, I looked back on some of the stuff I have written. Unfortunately, I concluded that, although we have made some progress in many areas, not much has changed socially. (Incidentally, I purposely chose not to include our pandemic-created status in my review.)

What I discovered was that we have made real progress in some areas of social concern, such as poverty and racism. But frankly, while some substantial changes have come about, some of that "progress" may be superficial. Sometimes we just "kicked the can on down the road" to somebody else: the next congress, school board, state legislature, the next county or town commission, and even to the next generation.

I have said many times that "everything in the world is personal." So I took a look back at what has changed for me in regard to those more regional, if not national and universal, concerns.

The biggest change I found was the influence of technology. Some of that is the result of just those very things the Lamar Society was proposing. Technology now dominates society. It has made communication of information, real or false, a part of every part of our lives for good or bad. If there is one we all have observed during this pandemic, it is how much we miss each other. Skype and Zoom and texting can't replace real personal contact. Just adding technology is not always progress.

None of the serious problems of racism, poverty, and education can be solved unless we talk to each other, not on the phone, not on Skype or Zoom, but in person. We Southerners pride ourselves on being "sociable." Sociability means putting ourselves in each other's shoes, seeing other viewpoints, so we really understand each other.

I don't know if the decrease in the number of small towns is progress. Big cities divide up into sections. In small towns, everybody lives together because we're too close to live apart.

I don't know if only looking to the future is the way to progress. Sometimes, it is important to look back. Some folks think we can change history by removing monuments and rewriting history books. Sometimes it is more important to know where you've been, to know about the good times and the bad and what caused both, so we can learn to build on both. We need to be aware of our mistakes, as well as our good choices.

To take my story a little closer to home, I have noted before that we don't have a county museum in Columbus County. The local depot museums do a great job of telling the story of their respective communities, but we don't have a collective repository for the history of this county. Much has happened here—some of it good and some of it not so good. All significant history didn't happen somewhere else. But who will know, without looking back, how to learn from our mistakes so we don't repeat them, how to build on our successes? That's impossible if we don't know where we've been and what we did. We need to know why and how we became who we are.

I have had many people of great accomplishment tell me that success in life is not a destination but a journey. I think the same thing applies to a community. How will we know the value of the journey if we don't know where we've been?

A Walk in the Woods

Every once in a while, I'll come across a place around here I haven't been. Such circumstance is becoming less and less likely as I get older and continue to travel 'round the county, gathering material for my stories about the various communities—most of which I have traveled to and written about for many years. But I found a road in the woods recently that I had never been down. It was just a small two-rutted road that led through the woods near the place where I had taken my wife for her weekly hair appointment. So while she was getting her hair done, I chose to explore that road.

It was just after noon when I started my exploration. The sun was shining, but there was a steady little breeze that moved the air around just enough to create a slight chill, enough to make me move along to the shelter of the trees where maybe I wouldn't feel the wind. That wasn't the case. The trees beside the road just channeled the wind.

The start of the road was a little uphill, not much, but enough to create little trenches formed by the frequent rain. Gravel had been hauled into that part of the road that had lessened the erosion, and the incline was so little it was almost imperceptible. I was off to a good start.

At the top of the incline was a grain bin and behind it the remnants of an old building with several discarded items around it. Age and weather had taken its toll on the old building which had served a purpose once as shelter and storage. It had collapsed under the weight of the circumstances.

The ruts in the road were more visible as I went farther down it. Most of the mudholes had dried up, but there was still enough mud to stick to my shoes and enough mudholes to make me move back and forth across the road to step on the drier places and on the leaves that covered the pathway.

A wire fence ran along one side of the road. There was a single strand of barbed wire at the top of the fence and typical old small-squared wire below it, all of it attached to posts that had begun to rot but still held the wire in place. The fence still served the purpose for which it was intended: to keep something in and/or out.

Somebody recently had mowed that road. The grass along the sides of the ruts was not very tall, and I could look through the woods on each side and see a blanket of fallen leaves that had kept the grass from growing in the woods. There were small saplings growing beside the bigger trees: sweet gum and pine and oak. As I looked up into the tall trees, I could see limbs, big and small, that had been broken away from the trunks of the trees by storms. But they had been caught in other, stronger limbs and, although they served no apparent useful purpose, still remained as a part of the forest.

There was a rusted gate open just around a curve in the road. Like the fence, its original purpose was to keep something in or out. But now it just hung there; its main function now was, apparently, to add some texture to the painting and make this road a little different from others. Suddenly, a pair of cardinals, a male and a female, silently flew over my head and landed on the rusty fence. The bright red mantle of the male contrasted with, yet matched, the rusty perch; the female's more subdued coat blended in with her resting place. Folklore says that cardinals are guardian angels, the spirit of loved ones who have passed now standing watch over us. I wondered why, with all the trees around, they chose the rusty fence. Everything serves a purpose.

And just past the gate, the road opened up a little. The road itself still was comprised of ruts leading to a field, but the roadside was wider, and I saw a small copse of longleaf pine, a rarity now even as it remains the symbol of the Old North State. I had to pick off a few needles to take home where I could measure them and put them with the others I have collected that have now turned brown with age.

The road disappeared into the field ahead. The field had been cleared and plowed and was ready to be planted once spring came. I don't know how long that spot of land had been cleared, but every year since that first cultivation, it was and has been the site of regeneration and renewal, a place where seeds can be planted and grow, plants will be tended and harvested, and the process repeated again. It's a reminder that life is a cyclical and productive process we can all survive despite whatever hardships we face.

I left the field behind me and started back. As I walked back down the same road I had just come, I saw the same things I had seen before, but I also saw some of them in a different light—from a different perspective—and I even saw things I had not seen before. In many ways, it was a lot like the road of life, where sometimes the signs and the experiences of the past are there, but we don't pay attention and learn from them until we travel that road again.

Looking for Peace and Quiet

At the end of a long day, have you ever said to yourself (or anyone within shouting distance), "I need a little peace and quiet"? Assuming you seek out a place where you can meet that need, where do you go?

There are a lot of advantages to living in Columbus County. One of them is the wide range of places that are quiet and peaceful. There also are some places that might be quiet and peaceful to some folks and not so to others. There is a difference between peace and quiet, and silence and loneliness.

So I set out on a journey, a quest, to find a place of peace and quiet I could use as a refuge from the rest of the world. That's when I found out that silence and seclusion are not the same as peace and quiet.

I drove over to the western part of the county where I knew there were a lot of roads with few houses. I figured the most quiet and peaceful place would be where there were the fewest people. (I had decided the Green Swamp would be a last resort, given the heat and mosquitoes.)

I had not gone far when I saw a wide-open expanse of green pasture that stretched so wide I couldn't see any trees over the horizon. The land belonged to a friend of mine. (I had decided I would trespass only on property of people I knew.) It was a bright, sunny day, not yet hot enough to be summer. I walked to the middle of the pasture and stopped on a hillock. There was a good breeze blowing. Through my hearing aids, it sounded like someone blowing on a microphone, so I took the aids out. It was a pleasant feeling standing there in the warmth of a summer day, breeze blowing just enough to keep the humidity from being a distraction. There were some cows in the distance not paying any attention to me. I thought how nice it would be to have nothing to do but eat and grow fat—no responsibilities, no cares. Then I remembered their eventual purpose, and I decided that cows didn't lead a perfect existence. It was peaceful and quiet in the pasture, but it wasn't a place where I felt I could truly relax since I was reluctant to sit down.

I got back in my car and headed down the road back toward Chadbourn. As I went around a curve, I saw an old tobacco barn on the side of the road. It had become covered in vines, and old pieces of tin had come lose and were flapping in the wind. It leaned precariously to one side. I stopped there on the ditch bank and got out of the car and looked at the old barn. It is a common sight now to see those old barns sinking into the past. I know it's trite and cliché to say, but standing there looking at that old barn, I could almost hear the chatter of workers "puttin' in" tobacco and smell that unique aroma as the green leaves turned to gold. It was peaceful and quiet, but it wasn't what I was looking for.

I drove on past my family's old farm and headed across the swamp toward Whiteville. I passed a large tract of land that recently had been covered in a stand of trees. Now it lay strewn with pieces of logs and logging debris. There was an old logging road that led from the highway into the cutover site. I turned in there, got out, and walked several yards across the fallen trees. Quiet. No breeze. The smell of turpentine. Pieces of old logs rotting in the sun. It was quiet there. It might have even been peaceful there, because I knew that the folks who owned that property were going to replant that whole acreage in pine trees. Another forest would grow there. I remembered my old days working for a paper company with the tagline, "Trees are a renewable resource." But I didn't feel the quiet; I felt the silence. So I went on down the road.

I went through Whiteville and Hillsboro and went by the baseball fields. I didn't stop, but I almost did. An empty athletic field is a quiet place because we associate it with sound—the sound of people. But when the people are gone, it is more than quiet. It is silent.

So I decided to go on down to Lake Waccamaw to the mouth of the river. It is always quiet there. And it was when I got there. I walked a few feet down the river—just a small little stream that would meander and widen all the way down to the Atlantic Ocean. You wouldn't think it much of a river right here at the lake. It was brown, not even two feet deep, and slowly moving through the shade of the cypress and sweet gum trees. The only sound was the water washing over the dam. *That* was peace and quiet. I began to feel I had reached my goal as I sat down on a fallen log there next to the river and watched a dragonfly (skeeter hawk) perch on the end of the log and a monarch butterfly tease him as the black-and-gold wings flitted over the still water. A heron strutted in the shallow water back toward the dam and was soon joined by two more feathered waders.

It was late afternoon as I sat there by the river, and some dark clouds already had covered the sun. I knew it was about to rain, but I didn't want to leave. So I stayed awhile longer. (Somebody told me once that I didn't have sense enough to get out of the rain!) The first raindrops came, little singular droplets that moved the leaves on the bushes around me. And still I sat there in the rain, watching the raindrops create circles on the river water. The wind picked up, creating a natural shower that washed away the heat and left in its wake a sense of peace. It wasn't quiet. I could hear the rain on the trees and hear the raindrops hit the water, and even when I heard the distant roll of thunder, it was a reassurance—not noise but God's whisper, "I got this."

I still haven't found the peace *and* the quiet. If you know a place I might try, tell me about it.

EPILOGUE

Almost every day, somebody will declare during any given year, "This year is the worst ever. I'll be glad when it's over." Not many will disagree, particularly regarding these last few years. The weather was terrible: a record number of hurricanes, torrential rains, and lots of flooding; an election season as stormy as any hurricane; and a pandemic that claimed millions of lives and changed the way we live.

To tell you the truth, I got tired of thinking about it. All the negativity was making me depressed and grumpy. So I decided I would consciously and deliberately look for some positivity. The first thing I thought of was something my mama used to tell me when I would get a case of "down in the dumps." "This too shall pass," she would say. Of course, Mama got that from the Bible. I think it was when the wise King Solomon, being asked for a verity, something undeniable, replied, "And this too shall pass away." And now it has been said many times by anonymous, as well as famous, people.

So I thought: *Well, maybe things aren't insurmountable. Things are gonna be brighter.* But being an English major is sometimes a curse. In the midst of optimism, I heard Macbeth in the depths of sorrow:

Tomorrow, and tomorrow, and tomorrow
Creeps on this petty pace from day to day ...
And all our yesterdays have lighted fools
The way to dusty death ...

It is a tale
Told by an idiot, full of sound and fury
Signifying nothing.

Old Macbeth thought life was meaningless after his wife died. He saw every day as being just like yesterday and the next day. Life had just beat him down. That kinda threw a wet blanket on my optimism.

But fortunately, my old English lit classes still lingered. I remember a portion of a poem called "Invictus" by William Ernest Henry. To be honest, I had to look up the author, and I have forgotten some of the words. But I remember this much:

It matters not how strait the gate,
How charged with punishments the scroll,
I am the master of my fate,
I am the captain of my soul.

I realized it was all up to me. I could let this mess around me overwhelm me, or I could keep looking for the positive no matter how hard it is to find. I realized we had a lot to be thankful for.

One of the things I am most thankful for is the opportunity to grow up in a small Southern town. Much of my old hometown has gone away—the people and the buildings. But the things I learned growing up here and living much of my adult live here still linger in my memory. More importantly, that place and that time became a part of me and hundreds of other people. And thousands of other people who lived in other small towns have taken their heritage and spread it around the world. Significance is relative. As for me, the small towns of this country are the basis of who we are. I hope we never forget that.

I realized something else too, something that every Southerner has as his mantra. I could hear Miz Scarlett in my mind: "After all, tomorrow is another day."

(Listen to Bill recite this poem, track number 9 on Just Down the Road.*)*

The Sigh of the South Wind

The sigh of the South Wind stills the night,
holding back the passing light
as music floats on lilting wings
and the nesting red bird sings.

The sea wind blows over shifting sands,
muting the music of the band,
and we dance in the breeze 'til our hearts take flight
and nestle there in the moonlight.

And small town girls on soft summer nights
paint young men's dreams that are daylight bright,
and promises dreamed and promises kept
are a part of tomorrow as each night they slept.

Faces fade and memories slip
like misty clouds 'round sailing ships,
places veiled with a mourning shawl
hiding times we can't recall.

We shared the light the sun would send;
we thought such light would never end.
But time prevailed and dreams took flight;
but, oh, it was a lovely light.

Acknowledgments

I wrote my first book, *Sweet Tea, Fried Chicken and Lazy Dogs,* back in 2003. It was about North Carolina. Twenty years later, I'm still writing about the Tar Heel state. Over the years, I have expanded my musings to include what I call My South, that geographic section of the United States that goes south from Maryland down to Florida and over to Texas. It's "My South" because I write about what is a part of me: the people, places, and events that have affected who I am. Each part of that area is distinctive, unique, but united in its diversity. It has been a pleasure to get to know the people and places and put my thoughts down on paper. Along the way, I had a lot of help, and this book is a great example of that assistance.

It is significant that this book, which will probably be my last, was written with the assistance of Mary Best, who edited my first one. Mary was the editor of *Our State* magazine and became the first editor of Mann Media Books, a part of the company that published the magazine. When I began work on this manuscript, Mary responded to my anxiety when the publishing business was faced with challenges of transportation and availability of materials, among other things, that would impair the timely publication of my book. She not only did her usual superb job of frankly addressing my effort but essentially became my de facto literary agent. I not only appreciate her help but cherish her friendship.

My cousin, Greg Thompson, set up my new website, www.southboundwithbillthompson.com, and my daughter, Mari, is now the website manager and booking agent. They do a great job.

Amy Ashby edited my previous book *Tuxedos and Pickup Trucks* as well as this one. I appreciate her help more than I can say. I need her considerable talents to keep me readable beyond Columbus County.

This collection of essays includes some commentary that I wrote for the *News Reporter* in Whiteville, North Carolina, *Our State* magazine, *Salt* magazine, and other publications that have generously allowed me to use them in this book.

The companion recording of *Just Down the Road* was a completely new experience for me. Mike Milligan and the musicians at Serenade Studios were wonderful. The music is more than accompaniment; it is part of the story.

My wife, Lynda, guarded the gate of phone calls so I could concentrate on my writing.

By far, my greatest influence in putting these stories together was the people of My South, particularly North Carolina. They not only let me through "The Gates of the City" to celebrate innumerable festivals with them, but they also let me into their clubs, churches, and businesses and even their homes. They let me become one of them, and that is the greatest honor I could receive.

Thank y'all.